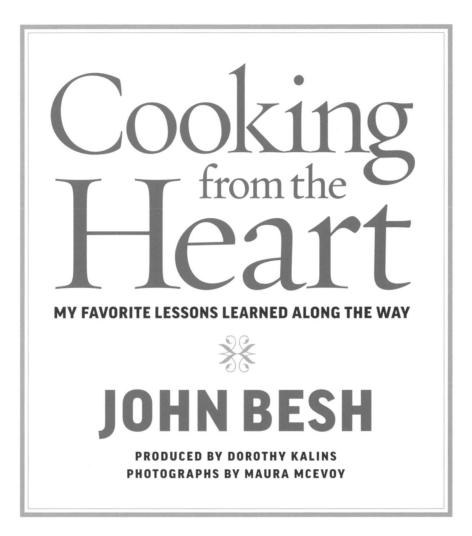

Cooking from the Heart

MY FAVORITE LESSONS LEARNED ALONG THE WAY

JOHN BESH

PRODUCED BY DOROTHY KALINS
PHOTOGRAPHS BY MAURA MCEVOY

Andrews McMeel
Publishing, LLC

Kansas City • Sydney • London

Cooking
from the
Heart

MY FAVORITE LESSONS LEARNED ALONG THE WAY

JOHN BESH

PRODUCED BY DOROTHY KALINS
PHOTOGRAPHS BY MAURA MCEVOY

ALSO BY JOHN BESH

My New Orleans: The Cookbook
200 of My Favorite Recipes & Stories from My Hometown, 2009

My Family Table
A Passionate Plea for Home Cooking, 2011

Andrews McMeel Publishing, LLC
an Andrews McMeel Universal company
1130 Walnut Street, Kansas City, Missouri 64106

www.andrewsmcmeel.com

www.chefjohnbesh.com

13 14 15 16 17 SDB 10 9 8 7 6 5 4 3 2 1

ISBN: 978-1-4494-3056-6

Library of Congress Control Number: 2013936654

Produced and edited by Dorothy Kalins,
Dorothy Kalins Ink, LLC

Book design: Don Morris, Don Morris Design

Photography: Maura McEvoy

Recipe editor: Sue Li

ATTENTION: SCHOOLS AND BUSINESSES

Andrews McMeel books are available at quantity discounts with bulk purchase for educational, business, or sales promotional use. For information, please e-mail the Andrews McMeel Publishing Special Sales Department: specialsales@amuniversal.com

Cooking from the Heart
*is dedicated to the many
passionate chefs who are
generous enough to
share, teach, and pass along
life lessons through food.*

———

*And to those cooks with the
humility to learn from them.*

vi

WHAT I LEARNED ALONG THE WAY

"Cooking from the Heart is more than a cookbook: it's a journey to revisit the places and the people from whom I've learned the most important cooking (and life) lessons."

I took this journey not just for the sake of nostalgia (though that was certainly part of it), but to clarify the meaning of cooking, for me and for you. I'm hoping that whether you're a home cook or a professional, you'll learn from the radiant recipes and cooking lessons on these pages. I certainly expect you to laugh at my follies and hope that they will keep you from making the same mistakes. Or at least that you'll have the good sense to make your own mistakes that are as memorable as mine.

Twenty years ago, after I had served in the Marines, graduated from the Culinary Institute of America, and cooked in the kitchens of some of the best Southern chefs, I somehow had the good fortune to know that I did not yet know enough. Fortune led me to extraordinary mentors, giving life to the adage: "When you're ready for a teacher, one will come along."

I thought I needed to go to France: Twenty years ago and especially for a cook from New Orleans, it was still the epitome of fine cooking. But I couldn't secure a paying internship, necessary since I had just married the girl of my dreams. Jenifer Berrigan, a brand-new law school graduate, had agreed to put her plans on hold to share this adventure with me. Family friends connected me with Karl-Josef Fuchs, the third-generation chef-owner of the Spielweg, then a Michelin-starred restaurant and hotel in the Black Forest in the loveliest, most gentle part of Germany. What I learned in that year at the Spielweg is revealed in the book's earliest chapters and easily summed up by this thought: Every time I thought I had something nailed, life had yet another surprising lesson just waiting for me around the next corner. Karl-Josef practices a community-based food culture that was decades ahead of America at the time. He was a formidable character to me then, but his ready good humor and incredible patience soon led to a deep friendship. As I write this, I realize I have since sent some eighteen of our cooks to learn in Karl-Josef's kitchen the way I was fortunate enough to do. Always, I urge them to explore, to taste, to travel, to get the hell out of their comfort zones. Curiosity, I believe, is a vital part of being a real cook.

Back in New Orleans, I found my second mentor, Chris Kerageorgiou, a fiery Frenchman who owned a restaurant called La Provence across Lake Pontchartrain in Lacombe, Louisiana. Chef Chris was something of a legend, drawing in curious diners with both the authenticity of his Provençal cooking and the pyrotechnics of his personality. Though by that time I thought I knew something about French cooking, Chef Chris decreed I did not and sent me to his tiny

Mediterranean town with these instructions: Breathe my air, shop my markets, befriend my butchers and bakers; learn to taste the way I taste! I fell hard for his Provence and managed to return often. Many years later, I was able to tell Chef Chris, as he was near death, that I would buy his restaurant, La Provence, and run it in the spirit of all he had taught me.

Chef Chris was instrumental in sending me to Rudy and Anne Baur at the Chateau de Montcaud, north of Avignon, where I agreed to cook a New Orleans–style jazz brunch for their sophisticated guests. Theirs was quite a different Provence and from Rudy, a worldly hotelier, I learned to cook with the kind of refinement that makes dining both a pleasure and an art. I was lucky enough to return to the Baurs for many summers thereafter, and later, to send some of my best cooks to apprentice there.

One day in the perfect town of St-Rémy-de-Provence, I walked into the restaurant of Alain Assaud, a man who had cooked with the loftiest chefs in France but left all that to open a small

WITH CHEF CHRIS and Joyce Bates, at La Provence, 1995. Right, at the Spielweg in 1993.

place in his hometown to cook his own way. I ate at Assaud's dozens of times before I went back to his small kitchen to ask him to teach me how to make his bouillabaisse. A fast friendship followed and it was one of the highlights of our book research to crowd into that same kitchen and capture the skill of Alain's hands and share the glow of his excitement as he prepared dishes that he's cooked a thousand times before.

These are some of the personalities who light up the pages of this book; people whose expertise and generosity have taught me lessons I will never forget. It is their voices I heard as I cooked each vivid recipe and made it my own. My hope is that this book will inspire you to cook my recipes and make them your own.

Cooking from the Heart tells my personal story: how cooking can go beyond mastering skills to become the passionate expression of a life; how I was forever changed by what I learned. In turn I hope I've inspired the hundreds of incredible cooks who followed me, encouraging them—and you—to find the soul in the food they make.

Lessons of

the Hunt

I

T IS A cold but beautiful grey day on the mountain slopes. I follow the old man closely, careful to step lightly into the crunchy snowpack from this first, very early snowfall, certain that the slightest squeak of my heavy leather boots will scare the *Reh,* the majestic roe deer we glimpse as we stalk him through the forest. Already he seems skittish after a couple hours of pursuit through the thick, dark, fairytale woods that are straight out of the Brothers Grimm. My heart is racing from the battle against Mother Gravity on the steep inclines of the Belchen, the fourth highest mountain in the German Black Forest. Those leather boots and my wool pants feel like they weigh as much as I do, but I don't mind. It seems I've spent a lifetime preparing for this moment.

THE MAGICAL MÜNSTER VALLEY, left, where the hamlet of Spielweg is nestled. Overleaf, Karl-Josef and his pals take a break at a favorite hunting spot, joined by Zorro the dog and chestnut Black Forest horses.

3

"My heart is racing, my boots and pants weigh as much as I do, but I don't mind. It seems I've spent a lifetime preparing for this moment."

FUCHS MEANS "FOX" in German, so foxes abound at the Spielweg, from left. My first snowy hunt with Karl-Josef in 1993. A natty K-J in his element. The lush facade of the Romantik Hotel Spielweg, below left.

the classic style of a Bergstutzen, a compact mountain rifle) and fitted with the best Austrian optics money can buy. A liver- and brown-colored Tyrolean hound of no small repute with, undoubtedly, a doctorate in hunting and a pedigree to match, waltzes silently alongside the old man (who is really only 32, 10 years younger than I am now, some 20 years later!). He is my chef, Karl-Josef Fuchs, a fearsome yet kind man with huge shoulders and a commanding stature that makes me want to follow him. In other words, I'm way the hell out of my league and loving every minute of it.

Out of nowhere, the *Reh* appears just yards from us, then bounds off. With the smoothness of a jazz musician, Karl-Josef stabs his stout hiking staff into the snow and, balancing expertly, lowers the rifle to rest on the staff, fitting the butt stock perfectly to his shoulder. Not a breath is taken. Then a gentle squeeze of the trigger releases the jarring, violent roar of the .300 Win Mag. Its energy drops the beautiful deer in its tracks, no more than 100 yards away. This is why he uses such a large cartridge, my chef explains: hunting is only ethical when one doesn't cause the animal any pain. A clean, ethical kill tastes better too; adrenaline gives the meat an undesirable musky flavor.

Mountain warfare as a Marine may have given me strength, but the desert (as in Desert Storm) never offered me such utter beauty, nor the fragrance of the pine boughs moving in the high mountain air. Nor did it allow for the sound of silence as we negotiate the rough terrain, trying to outwit and harvest this deer as he glides effortlessly through thick alder and *Tannenbaum,* guarded by several smaller bucks who act as sentries, ready to signal alarm.

I feel just as I did at seven or eight years old, following my father and grandfather through Louisiana's low-lying cypress swamps and the jagged red clay hills planted in pine, chasing after our elusive whitetail deer. I was reared to pursue the art of hunting with bows, arrows, shotguns, and rifles. The meat my family ate during hunting season was wild. So I could have approached this day in the Black Forest as just another hunt. But as my perspiration-soaked green felt hat suggests, I am experiencing a major case of nervous anticipation, knowing that around the next corner a beautiful deer might just allow me to take a clean, ethical shot. My mind races as I run through scenarios in which my chef would hand me the rifle to take the shot. The rifle itself gives me a case of the willies; it's the most gorgeous weapon—a piece of art meticulously engraved and hand-forged by master craftsmen, each of its two barrels a different caliber (in

Without wasting time, my chef carefully removes his small, stag-horned knife from a tiny pocket on the side of his lederhosen. He slices a small branch from a fir tree and briskly approaches the felled animal, opens its mouth, and inserts the branch. Eyes closed, he quietly prays over the deer. Later, he'll tell me that the evergreen will feed the soul of the animal in eternity. With such care given to every aspect of the harvest, I know that cooking it will be inspiring. But before we can do that, our *Reh* must be properly field dressed, the entrails removed, and the heart, liver, and kidneys cared for.

5

These organs, Karl-Josef explains, are the prize. As for the rest of the magnificent beast, it will hang in the meat locker outside the kitchen for up to seven days.

Word of our fruitful hunt doesn't take long to get out and by the time we return home to the Spielweg (the restaurant where I am interning for a year), Coco, the local wild game inspector, is there waiting in the pristine, white-tiled kitchen, microscope in hand. I laugh to myself, imagining a USDA meat inspector showing up to take tissue samples of our wild game minutes before we serve it to paying guests! Coco does his thing and then settles in to enjoy his schnapps and listen to tales of the hunt. The usual suspects who drink nightly in our employee dining room had shown up earlier in the day; now the farmers and neighbors and fellow hunters make their way to the open window that graces the *garde manger* kitchen, primed for a morsel of the preparation Karl-Josef will dream up for his fresh venison liver. As they knock back juice cups of Markgräfler, the local red wine, the jovial entourage grows ever more boisterous, making me realize that such post-hunt gatherings are woven thick into the fabric of life here in this tiny mountain hamlet.

The butchery won't happen for a while, yet the chef wastes no time in carefully trimming and removing each thread of sinuous connective tissue attached to the venison liver. Gripping the well-worn wooden handle of an incredibly sharp carbon steel butcher's knife, he slices the liver into half-inch escalopes on an old walnut butcher's block. He seasons each slice with a touch of flaky sea salt and a light grating from a whole nutmeg, then delicately places the liver in a very heavy, hot, buttered *sautoir* and cooks it over high heat to a perfect medium rare, using a silver serving spoon to bathe each slice with sizzling hot butter. As the slices are done, he removes them from the pan to rest momentarily, then sautés thinly sliced onions with small diced bright yellow potatoes and diced quince—*Bratkartoffeln*—that becomes florally aromatic as it softens in the pan.

"My chef slices the liver on an old walnut butcher's block, seasons each slice with a touch of flaky sea salt, and delicately places them in a very heavy, hot, buttered sautoir."

The chef serves each medium-rare slice of venison liver over the potatoes and quince, finishing the dish with a few pinches of chives chopped to a uniform fineness. He adds just a slight drizzle of local aged honey vinegar, a sweet tartness that perfectly balances the warm fatty liver, the quince-infused *Bratkartoffeln,* and a petite salad of lamb's lettuce dressed with pumpkin seed oil. How, I think, could meager venison liver be so memorable? As I inhale my portion, I reflect on the magical day afield, keenly aware that I was in the right place, not just among enthusiastic hunters and cooks, but with a chef/teacher who inspires me to handle food with a reverence that is spiritual.

NEWLYWED JENIFER and the farmhouse where we rented a room, 1993, left. Yvonne in the dining room, above. With our old VW Jetta on a typical snowy morning, below. A photo of Karl-Josef and his brothers hangs in the restaurant.

VENISON LIVER WITH HONEY VINEGAR GLAZE

Serves 4–6

1 pound venison or calves' liver, thinly sliced

Salt

Pinch freshly ground nutmeg

4 tablespoons butter

1 onion, thinly sliced

1 yellow potato, peeled and diced

1 quince (or apple), peeled and diced

Freshly ground black pepper

2 tablespoons chopped fresh chives

2 tablespoons honey vinegar

4 cups mâche

2 teaspoons pumpkin seed oil

1 teaspoon sherry vinegar

IF YOU ARE LUCKY ENOUGH to get your hands on some venison liver, this is one of the best ways to enjoy it. But substituting calves' liver does not mean losing the experience of the dish, so go ahead and try it. If honey vinegar is difficult to find, just mix equal parts honey and cider vinegar. I serve this as Karl-Josef does with *Bratkartoffeln,* sautéed potatoes and quince (page 94).

1. Season the liver slices on both sides with salt and nutmeg. Melt the butter in a large cast iron skillet over medium-high heat. When the butter is foamy, add the liver slices and quickly sear, about 30 seconds a side. Do this in batches so you're searing, not steaming, the liver. While cooking, tilt the pan so that the butter pools at the edge and, with a metal spoon, ladle it over the liver. Transfer the liver to a platter.

2. Add the onion, potato, and quince to the same skillet and cook until the potato and quince are tender, about 10 minutes. Season with salt and pepper.

3. Sprinkle the liver slices with the chives and drizzle with the honey vinegar. In a large bowl, dress the mâche with the pumpkin seed oil and vinegar and season with salt. Serve the liver with the greens and potatoes and quince.

CHARCUTERIE doesn't get more authentic than this. Clockwise from left, Rabbit in Gelée with Chanterelles, Boar's Head Pâté, Duck Confit, Country Pâté, Sülze, cured bacon, Duck Liver Mousse, and Schmaltz.

PORK LIVER PÂTÉ

Makes 1 small terrine

1 tablespoon olive oil

1 medium onion, chopped

2 cloves garlic, minced

1 pound pork belly, finely ground

8 ounces pork liver, finely ground

8 ounces pork shoulder, finely ground

1 teaspoon My Four Spice Mix, right

½ teaspoon ground coriander

1 tablespoon pink curing salt

Leaves from 3 sprigs fresh thyme, chopped

Salt

I LIKE TO FUNNEL THIS MIXTURE into a bologna casing and then poach it at a very low simmer, which results in a lovely cylinder of pâté. You can certainly make it like that, but it's much easier to cook it the way we prepare our other pâtés: baked in a small terrine in a water bath. The terrine makes rectangular, not round, slices, but that's the only difference.

1. Preheat the oven to 325°. Heat the oil in a medium skillet over medium heat. Add the onions and garlic and cook until translucent, about 5 minutes.

2. Combine the ground pork belly, liver, and shoulder in the bowl of a stand mixer fitted with a paddle. Mix until it pulls away from the sides of the bowl. (Or mix it vigorously by hand in a large bowl.) Add the cooked onions and garlic, the Four Spice Mix, coriander, and pink salt. Continue to mix until the seasonings are evenly distributed. Stir in the thyme and season with salt.

3. Test the seasoning by frying a spoonful of the meat mixture in a skillet over high heat. Taste, and if you think it needs it, add a bit more salt or spice.

4. Spoon the pork mixture into a small terrine. Place the terrine in a large roasting pan and add enough hot water to reach halfway up the sides. Bake, uncovered, until the internal temperature reaches 140°, about 1 hour. Let cool, then slice in the terrine and serve.

MY FOUR SPICE MIX

QUATRE ÉPICES is a classic French seasoning combination, often used in charcuterie and hearty soups and stews. It's usually made from ground, toasted peppercorns, ginger, nutmeg, and cloves. If I can't get my hands on the original Quatre Épices Bovida, which is still sold today, I'll just toast and grind the spices and keep the mix in a small jar. My go-to recipe is this:

1 heaping tablespoon black peppercorns

2 teaspoons whole cloves

2 teaspoons ground ginger

1 teaspoon freshly ground nutmeg

GELATIN THOUGHTS

• **AT HOME I USE** powdered gelatin, an easy-to-use form of animal collagen, which comes in handy quarter-ounce packets equal to about 1 tablespoon.

• Always dissolve gelatin first in cold water to let the powder expand for a few minutes, then stir the dissolved gelatin into hot liquid. Never boil the gelatin, boiled gelatin will not set!

• One packet of gelatin will set 2 cups liquid firmly, 3 cups softly.

• Don't freeze liquids with gelatin in them or you'll have a curdled mess once thawed.

• You'll notice that some of these recipes require more gelatin than others. That's because meats like whole chickens, bone-in pork and veal have lots of natural collagen that helps stiffen the aspic. Pheasant and rabbit have less collagen, so you'll need to use a bit more gelatin.

RABBIT IN GELÉE WITH CHANTERELLE SALAD

Makes 8–10 ramekins

1 young rabbit
(about 3 pounds)

1 onion, chopped

1 leek, chopped

2 carrots, diced small

1 sprig fresh thyme

1 bay leaf

2 cloves

1 teaspoon crushed
coriander seeds

Pinch freshly
grated nutmeg

Pinch cayenne
pepper

8 cups Basic Chicken
Stock (page 250)

Salt

1 cup diced
celery root

3 tablespoons
chopped fresh
chives

2 packets
(.25 ounce each)
powdered gelatin

Freshly ground
black pepper

About 2 cups
small chanterelle
mushrooms

A handful of cherry
tomatoes, halved

Olive oil

Sherry vinegar

HERE'S ONE WAY TO THINK ABOUT A GELÉE: individual ramekins used as molds to turn out little aspics with morsels of rabbit and diced vegetables. I like to serve this appetizer with a beautiful salad of chanterelles and cherry tomatoes to enhance the delicate flavor of the rabbit. Or serve it more simply, with a variety of pickled vegetables.

1. Combine the rabbit, onions, leeks, half the carrots, the thyme, bay leaf, cloves, coriander, nutmeg, cayenne, and Chicken Stock in a large, heavy-bottomed pot. Season with salt and bring to a boil over high heat. Reduce the heat to low, cover, and simmer slowly for 1½ hours. Transfer the rabbit to a bowl.

2. Strain the cooking liquid through a fine-mesh sieve into a medium pot and discard the aromatics. Bring the stock to a gentle boil, reduce the heat, and simmer, uncovered, until it has reduced by about half to 3–4 cups, about 30 minutes. Remove from the heat and add the remaining carrots, the celery root, and the chives. Soften the gelatin in ½ cup cold water and let sit for

10 minutes. Add the gelatin to the reduced stock and stir until dissolved.

3. Debone the rabbit and dice the meat, then add it to the stock. Season with salt and pepper. Taste and if you think it needs it, add more salt and pepper.

4. Evenly divide the rabbit, vegetables, and stock among 8 or 10 ramekins. Refrigerate until set, at least 2 hours. Meanwhile, toss chanterelles and tomatoes with oil and vinegar and reserve.

5. To serve, place the ramekins in a pan of warm water for just a moment to soften the gelée. Use a knife to release, then invert, and carefully unmold onto a plate.

COUNTRY PÂTÉ

Makes 1 generous terrine

5 slices white bread, torn

¾ cup whole milk

1½ pounds lean ground pork

1 pound ground pork fat

1 egg

1 teaspoon My Four Spice Mix (page 12)

Salt

Freshly ground black pepper

8 ounces chicken livers

½ cup Armagnac

8 ounces pork fatback, skin removed, diced small

4 ounces pork fatback, thinly sliced by your butcher, or caul fat

4 bay leaves

4 sprigs fresh thyme

1 packet (.25 ounce) powdered gelatin

2 cups Basic Chicken Stock (page 250)

THIS IS MY FAVORITE rustic country-style pâté. It's important to be true to the proportions of liver, fat, and ground pork; however the *kinds* of meat or fat are easily substituted. Wild boar or venison work beautifully in place of the pork, and chicken, duck, or pork livers are interchangeable. After it's baked, I like to baste the pâté with aspic, which adds moisture and makes it less crumbly.

1. Mix together the bread and milk in a medium bowl and set aside until the bread has soaked up all the milk, about 30 minutes.

2. Preheat the oven to 300°. In a large mixing bowl, blend the ground meat with the ground pork fat, egg, Four Spice Mix, and the soaked bread. Season with salt and pepper. Mix energetically into a creamy texture. Add the chicken livers, the Armagnac, and about ¼ cup ice water, and continue to mix. Season with salt and pepper.

3. Test the seasoning by frying a spoonful of the meat mixture in a skillet over high heat. Taste, and if you think it needs it, add a bit more salt or spice. Fold in the diced fatback.

4. Line a large terrine with the sliced fatback, letting it hang over the sides by at least 2 inches. Spoon the meat mixture into the terrine. Lay the bay leaves and thyme sprigs over the top, then cover with the overhanging fatback.

5. Place the terrine in a large roasting pan and add enough hot water to reach halfway up the sides. Bake until the internal temperature of the pâté reaches 140°, 35–40 minutes.

6. While the terrine is baking, make the aspic. Soften the gelatin in ¼ cup cold water for 10 minutes. Bring the Chicken Stock to a boil, turn off the heat, and stir in the gelatin until completely dissolved. Set aside.

7. Carefully remove the terrine from the water bath and let it to cool to room temperature so that the fats and juices from the meat are reabsorbed. While the terrine is cooling, baste it with a couple of tablespoons of aspic every 10 or 15 minutes, until you've used all the aspic. Once the terrine has cooled completely, cover and refrigerate overnight.

8. To serve, slice the terrine right in the pan. It will keep in the refrigerator for about a week.

1. Measure each ingredient in a separate bowl. Combine the ground pork and ground pork fat in a mixing bowl.

2. Mix together the soaked bread and the spice mix with the pork. Add the egg and season with salt and pepper.

5. Test for seasoning by frying a spoonful of the pâté mixture. Taste and add more salt and spice mix if needed.

6. Fold the diced fat into the mixed and seasoned pâté. You'll want to see the fat in the finished slices.

3. Now mix the ingredients in the bowl together energetically to soften the fat and create a creamy texture.

4. Add the chicken liver and just enough ice water to chill the mixture. Mix vigorously into a smooth paste.

7. Line the terrine with sliced fatback, letting it hang over the sides by at least 2 inches. Fold in the mixture.

8. Lay the thyme and bay leaves over the pâté and gently fold the fatback over to completely cover the terrine.

TERRINE OF RARE DUCK BREAST & RILLETTES

Makes 1 generous terrine

1 whole star anise

½ teaspoon whole coriander

1 teaspoon My Four Spice Mix (page 12)

1 packet (.25 ounce) powdered gelatin

1 cup Basic Chicken Stock (page 250)

Salt

8 wild duck breasts (or 6 domestic duck breasts, sliced in half horizontally), skinned

2 teaspoons sugar

2 cups duck fat, melted

2 shallots, chopped

1 clove garlic, minced

½ cup Madeira

3 cups shredded Duck Confit (page 23)

Leaves from 6 sprigs fresh thyme, chopped

½ small bunch fresh chives, chopped

Freshly ground black pepper

Oil, for brushing

I LOVE TO MAKE THIS TERRINE with the tiny wild duck breasts from birds we hunt. However, I realize you'll probably do *your* hunting in the supermarket and come up with the much meatier domestic duck breasts. In that case, be sure to remove the fatty skin (which you can render later for luscious duck fat), and carefully slice each breast in half horizontally, so that they sear quickly and absorb the flavorful seasonings of the rillettes (made from shredded Duck Confit, page 23) as the terrine chills.

1. Toast the star anise, coriander, and Four Spice Mix in a small skillet over medium heat until fragrant. Finely grind in a spice grinder. Reserve.

2. For the aspic, soften the gelatin in ¼ cup cold water for 10 minutes. Bring the Chicken Stock to a boil in a small saucepan and turn off the heat. Stir in the gelatin until completely dissolved. Season with salt and reserve.

3. Liberally season each duck breast with the spice mixture, sugar, and salt. Heat 2 tablespoons of the duck fat in a large skillet over medium-high heat. Working in batches, sear the duck breasts until browned, about 2 minutes each side. Transfer to a plate and reserve.

4. Add 2 tablespoons of the duck fat to the same large skillet and reduce the heat to medium. Add the shallots and garlic and cook until the shallots are translucent, 2–3 minutes. Add the Madeira and cook until the mixture is syrupy, 3–5 minutes.

5. In a food processor, make the rillettes by blending together the Madeira mixture, the Duck Confit, and thyme. With the processor still running, drizzle in the remaining melted duck fat and the aspic. Add the chives and season with salt and pepper.

6. Brush a large terrine with oil and line with plastic wrap. Fill the bottom of the terrine with about a ½-inch layer of the rillettes, smoothing with a rubber spatula. Next make a layer of seared duck breasts. Repeat the layering process until all the duck is used, making sure a layer of rillettes is on top. Cover the terrine with plastic wrap and chill overnight before serving. It will keep in the refrigerator for a week.

MY KARL-JOSEF

A Toast to My Chef: Dinner at the Spielweg, September 3, 2012

CHARLIE OVER HERE will have to translate for everybody because Karl-Josef will never translate me correctly! The reason we're here is that when I worked at the Spielweg twenty years ago, I was so impressed and learned so much. I grew up as a hunter, and here I cooked for hunters. Not only did I work for Karl-Josef in his kitchen, he took me into his family and invited me to sit with them at the *Stammtisch—* the family table. But it wasn't just his personality and his obviously handsome good looks that impressed me as much as his understanding of what was really important in life—his family and his community.

It seemed to me that Karl-Josef managed everything perfectly. I had never worked for a chef who had balance. The chefs I worked for were always crazy. Now Karl-Josef is a little crazy. And I know he hunts *a lot*. But personally, I think that's a great thing. Hence, I want to be like Karl-Josef one day. Finding balance in life was really hard for me, because up until then I'd never seen anybody with Karl-Josef's kind of balance. Looking at him forced me to confront myself. He inspired me to be a husband first, then a father, and then a chef. (Usually, it's the other way around.) The chefs I worked for all had three, or four, or five wives and never got around to having a family. Karl-Josef was the one who really inspired me to be a better person.

I treasure the way he made connections with everybody in the community, from Max, the dairy farmer, who we buy milk from to make the cheese, to the potato farmer across the valley, and the local trout fisherman. Karl-Josef's idea of a food community was so far ahead of its time. Now, at last, we're seeing major progress: people everywhere are honoring local artisans, like those of you here in the Spielweg community who are so important. The people who raise the pork for the ham, Phillipp Schladerer over there, who makes such refined fruit schnapps. Martin Wassmer right here, who grows the grapes and turns them into such lovely wines. I believe that Karl-Josef really led the way in supporting this kind of food community.

Calling him a German chef really doesn't do him justice. He is so much bigger than that. Which is good, because unfortunately we think of German food the way we think of American food. When I say I'm a chef, I don't mean I'm an American chef, I mean I'm a chef from New Orleans, or from Louisiana. I try to share my culture through my food in the same way that Karl-Josef taught me to do so many years ago.

What I learned here in 1993 and 1994 plays a big part in my success today. It's why these books (*My New Orleans* and *My Family Table*), are doing so well and why we're here in Münstertal creating our third book, which I think I'll call *My Karl-Josef!* So here's to my mentor and my chef, Herr Fuchs!

TERRINE OF DUCK LIVER MOUSSE

Makes 1 small terrine

2 pounds duck livers

2 cups whole milk

1¼ cups duck fat, melted

1 onion, diced

2 small apples, peeled and diced

Salt

Freshly ground black pepper

1 teaspoon My Four Spice Mix (page 12)

¼ teaspoon ground coriander

Pinch cayenne pepper

½ cup ruby port

3 eggs, at room temperature

THIS VERY REFINED, SMOOTH-TEXTURED PÂTÉ is an elegant way to begin a meal. You can substitute rabbit, chicken, or even pork livers, or a mixture of those, as long as the proportions of the ingredients remain the same. It is really easier to make than you might think. Like any of these pâtés, it can be made a day or two before a big dinner. Not only does the taste improve, but you've spread out the prep work.

1. Submerge the livers in the milk in a large bowl, cover, and refrigerate for a few hours.

2. Preheat the oven to 300°. Heat 1 tablespoon of the duck fat in a large skillet over moderate heat. Add the onions and apples and cook until translucent and tender, 7–10 minutes. Season with salt and pepper and transfer to a blender.

3. Drain the livers, pat dry, and season with the Four Spice Mix, coriander, cayenne, and salt. Add a couple tablespoons of duck fat to the same large skillet and raise the heat to high. In batches, add the livers and sear, turning, until they become mahogany brown but are still rare inside, just about 30 seconds. Transfer the livers to the blender.

4. Deglaze the skillet with the port, scraping up any brown bits with a wooden spoon, and cook 2–3 minutes. Transfer to the blender, add the eggs, and blend on high until smooth. Drizzle in the remaining melted duck fat and continue to blend until fully incorporated.

5. Test the seasoning by frying a spoonful of the meat mixture in a skillet over high heat. Taste, and if you think it needs it, add a bit more salt or spice.

6. Press the liver mixture through a fine-mesh strainer into a small terrine. Transfer the terrine to a large roasting pan and add enough hot water to reach halfway up the terrine. Bake, uncovered, until the internal temperature reaches 140°, about 30 minutes.

7. Remove the mousse from the terrine and let cool. Cover and refrigerate until chilled. Serve the mousse in generous slices with toasted bread.

DUCK CONFIT

Makes 6 legs

6 duck legs and
thighs

Salt

Freshly ground
black pepper

1 clove garlic,
thinly sliced

2 sprigs fresh thyme

6 bay leaves

4-6 cups duck fat

CONFIT—SLOW-ROASTED DUCK STORED IN ITS OWN FAT—is an ancient way to preserve duck. I love serving these hot, crispy duck legs with anything from a hearty salad with a bracing vinaigrette, to luscious lentils, to sautéed apples or Sautéed Potatoes with Quince & Onions (page 94). I also use this confit to make rillettes (boneless confit emulsified with warm duck fat) that are then layered with thin slices of duck breast to create a terrine, essentially using every part of the bird in one dish (Terrine of Rare Duck Breast & Rillettes, page 18).

1. Liberally season the duck legs all over with salt and pepper. Tuck a slice of garlic, a small branch of thyme, and a bay leaf on the flesh-side of each leg and lay in a large baking dish. Cover with plastic wrap and refrigerate overnight.

2. Preheat the oven to 325°. Melt the duck fat in a medium saucepan over medium heat. Pour the melted fat over the duck legs in the baking dish so that they are completely submerged. Slow-roast in the oven until the legs are fork tender, about

2 hours. Let the duck cool in the fat. When the legs and fat are cool, cover and refrigerate overnight.

3. To serve the duck confit, preheat the oven to 375°. Remove the duck legs from the fat and place on a baking pan fitted with a wire rack. Bake until the skin is crispy and the legs are heated through, 25–30 minutes. Strain the remaining duck fat into a jar, refrigerate, and use for crispy fried potatoes.

PHEASANT IN GELÉE WITH SHALLOT VINAIGRETTE

Serves 6

1 3-pound pheasant

10 cups Basic Chicken Stock (page 250)

1 onion, chopped

2 carrots, diced

1 stalk celery, diced

½ small celery root, peeled and diced

2 packets (.25 ounce each) powdered gelatin

2 tablespoons chopped fresh chives

FOR THE SHALLOT VINAIGRETTE

1 shallot, minced

1 clove garlic, minced

3 tablespoons cider vinegar

6 tablespoons hazelnut or walnut oil

2 pinches sugar

Salt

Freshly cracked black pepper

A few handfuls salad greens

THE GREAT THING ABOUT THIS DISH (besides its obvious beauty) is that so much of it can be made in advance; it's a wonderful appetizer for a dinner party. You can serve it right in the bowls you make it in (clear glass makes all the difference) and garnish at the last minute with bright salad greens and the sharp vinaigrette.

1. Rinse and pat the pheasant dry. In a large heavy-bottomed pot, combine the pheasant, Chicken Stock, onions, half the carrots, and the celery and bring to a boil over high heat. Reduce the heat, cover, and simmer until the pheasant is tender but not falling off the bones, about 1 hour. Transfer the pheasant to a platter.

2. Strain the cooking liquid through a fine-mesh strainer into a medium pot and discard the vegetables. Bring the stock to a gentle boil, reduce the heat, and simmer, uncovered, until it has reduced by half to about 5 cups, about 30 minutes. Add the remaining carrots and the celery root and remove the pot from the heat. Soften the gelatin in ½ cup cold water and let sit for 10 minutes. Add the gelatin to the hot stock and stir until completely dissolved.

3. Skin and debone the cooked pheasant, then cut into small pieces.

4. Evenly divide the cooked pheasant among 6 small bowls. Sprinkle with the chopped chives and ladle the warm gelatin broth and vegetables over the pheasant. Refrigerate the bowls until the aspic is set and you're ready to serve, at least 2 hours.

5. Make the Shallot Vinaigrette by whisking all ingredients together in a small bowl.

6. To serve, scatter the salad greens over the bowls and dress with the Shallot Vinaigrette.

SÜLZE: PORK HEAD CHEESE

Makes 1 small terrine

3 pigs' feet

8 ounces pork shoulder

1 leek, white parts diced, greens chopped and reserved

2 carrots, diced small

1 cup diced celery root

4 cloves garlic, peeled and crushed

1 tablespoon salt, plus more for seasoning

1 teaspoon black peppercorns

1 teaspoon crushed red pepper flakes

1 bay leaf

2 sprigs fresh thyme

16 cups Basic Chicken Stock (page 250)

1 packet (.25 ounce) powdered gelatin

Oil, for brushing

MANY BUTCHERS CARRY CASINGS FOR CHARCUTERIE. The *Sülze* is then easily spooned into the casing and chilled; when you're ready to serve it, just remove the casing and slice into rounds. But I often make this head cheese in a terrine, which is easier. The traditional recipe calls for a whole hog's head—not easy to find. But if you're up for it, by all means search one out and substitute it for the pigs' feet and pork shoulder (cooking it a few hours longer).

1. In a large heavy-bottomed pot, combine the pigs' feet, pork shoulder, leek whites, half the carrots, half the celery root, the garlic, salt, peppercorns, red pepper, bay leaf, and thyme. Add the Chicken Stock and bring to a boil over high heat. Reduce the heat to low and simmer, uncovered, for 2–2½ hours. Remove the pigs' feet and pork to a bowl. Strain the stock through a fine-mesh sieve.

2. Return 1 quart of the stock to the cleaned pot. Add the remaining carrots and celery root and the leek greens. Bring to a boil and remove from the heat. Soften

the gelatin in ¼ cup cold water and let sit for 10 minutes. Add the gelatin to the hot stock and stir until dissolved. Set aside.

3. Pull the pork from the bones and dice. Brush a small terrine with oil and line with a large sheet of plastic wrap. Add the meat and the stock to the terrine and cover it completely with another sheet of plastic wrap. Chill the terrine overnight.

4. To serve, lift the *Sülze* out of the terrine and onto a board. Unwrap and slice.

SCHMALTZ WITH APPLES & ROSEMARY

Makes 1 small bowl

3 pounds pork belly, cut into small chunks

2 onions, peeled and quartered

4 cloves garlic, peeled and smashed

2 apples, cored and quartered

2 sprigs fresh rosemary

Salt

Freshly ground black pepper

I LEARNED THE LESSON WELL at the Spielweg that nothing, and I mean nothing, should go to waste. This includes the fat of any animal. We're so used to thinking of the word *schmaltz* as chicken fat, but in the Black Forest any rendered animal fat is schmaltz, and can be highly seasoned and used as a spread. This recipe originally called for wild boar bellies, which are almost impossible to come by.
But I like to make schmaltz from good-quality pork belly or even from those fatty, farm-raised duck skins.

1. Combine the pork belly, onions, garlic, apples, and 4 cups water in a large heavy-bottomed pot and bring to a boil over high heat. Reduce the heat to medium low and slowly simmer for 45 minutes. Add the rosemary and reduce the heat to low. Simmer until the water has evaporated and the rendered fat is clear and slightly bubbly, about 1 hour.

2. Strain the rendered fat through a fine-mesh strainer into a bowl and season with salt and pepper. Chill. Serve on warm, crusty bread.

I MEET THE WILD BOAR
My Mentor Had a Blow Torch in His Hand and Dinner on His Mind

THE SEPTEMBER DAY THAT I ARRIVED at the Spielweg to photograph for this book, I was not surprised to discover Karl-Josef had a beautiful *wilde Sau* in the meat locker, waiting for me to help butcher. I had just traveled what seemed like around the world, two days earlier evacuating my wife, four boys, and two dogs from our Hurricane Isaac–flooded house by wooden pirogue, and finally managing to get out of New Orleans. Three airplanes and a four-hour drive from Frankfurt later, I was greeted by my mentor with a blow torch in his hand, all the better to burn the hair from the wild boar he had shot in the Black Forest. Completely exhausted and emotionally frayed, this was the perfect therapy after such a journey.

Although Karl-Josef is an avid hunter, managing the wild boar population in the high alpine pastures that surround the Spielweg is far from frivolous blood sport. Wild boar are notorious for vandalizing those pastures, tearing up the delicious mountain grasses by their very roots. Those grasses are crucial to supporting the local dairy farmers (such milk, such cheese!) and their prized Hinterwälder cattle. Many's the lunch hour I gave up as a young cook to help our farmer neighbors by shoveling dirt into trenches made by those mischievous swine.

Of course I know full well that most of us do not have (or will ever have) access to the head of a wild boar to turn into pâté. And I did hesitate for a moment about whether to include Karl-Josef's specialty in this book. Sure, this is a remarkably intense procedure, but it is probably the best example of the deep authenticity of Karl-Josef's cooking philosophy that has influenced me so dramatically. And that, I decided, was reason enough. (Just reading the recipe is fun, even if you go no further.) Karl-Josef credits the recipe itself to the great early-nineteenth-century French chef, Antonin Carême, who served boar's head pâté slow-cooked as Karl-Josef does, stuffed with a couple of pounds of black truffles (which my chef substitutes with wild mushrooms). If you have both the time and inclination to devote to this

incredible pâté, consider using a domestic, sustainably raised pig's head and its parts, which are findable if you know a good butcher. Or farmer. You'll have to forego, however, my favorite step: the archaic torching and singeing of the hair of the animal, which renders the head smooth as a football and ready for stuffing. The rest is pretty straightforward, using a pork shoulder that is mixed and seasoned like a country pâté, and piling it into the head, which becomes its terrine.

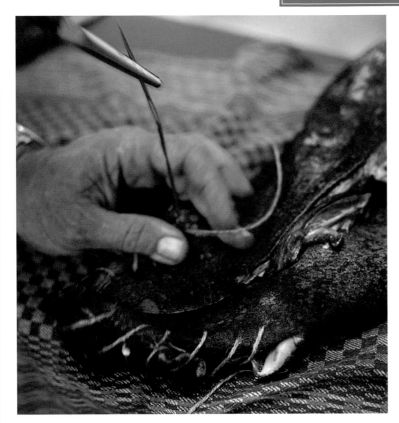

1. Make a container for the pâté by sewing together the skin of the boar's head with a strong needle and twine.

2. Use a meat grinder to process the head and shoulder meat, pork fat, and green onions and season with spices.

3. Wrap the stuffed head in a large cloth dish towel or layered cheesecloth and tie with butchers' twine.

4. After slow-cooking, refrigerate the pâté overnight, then unwrap and slice as thinly as possible.

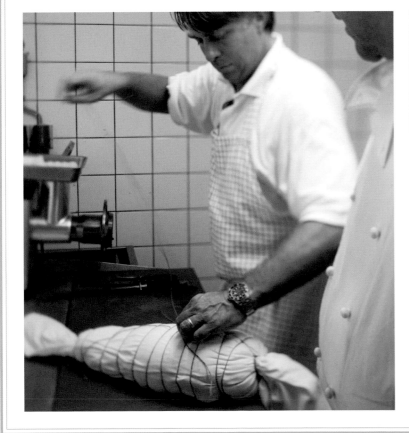

KARL-JOSEF'S WILD BOAR'S HEAD PÂTÉ

Serves 12–18

1 heart, cut into small chunks

1 tongue, cut into small chunks

¼ cup pink curing salt

1 wild boar's head, hair removed, or a pig's head

3 pounds shoulder meat

2 pounds pork fat

1 bunch green onions, chopped

¼ cup Calvados

1 tablespoon ground white pepper

½ teaspoon ground coriander

½ teaspoon ground nutmeg

½ teaspoon ground mace

½ cup toasted pistachios

½ cup black trumpet or wild mushrooms

4 calves' feet

½ cup white wine vinegar

½ cup white wine

1 bay leaf

CERTAINLY NOT FOR THE FAINT OF HEART, making this pâté might seem daunting and slightly out-there, but it does capture the spirit of the hunt and the spirit of the Spielweg by using every part of the animal. And if you are ever going to attempt such a feat, why not do it the proper way? If you were to substitute the head and parts of a correctly raised pig, the resulting pâté would be every bit as worthwhile. The point here is that nothing goes to waste and, through revering these off-cuts, delicious charcuterie is born.

1. In a medium bowl, combine the heart and tongue and sprinkle with 1 tablespoon of the pink curing salt. Cover and marinate in the refrigerator overnight.

2. Debone the head by turning it over and making an incision underneath the lower jaw, carefully removing the skin and meat from the skull. Be careful not to cut through the skin as it will be the cooking vessel of this pâté. Scrape away all meat from the head, including the delicious cheeks to use in the pâté. The skull can be used for stock.

3. Sew the skin of the head back together with a large needle and butcher's twine, starting at the tip of the snout and stitching along the sides. The key here is to stitch the head together so that it can be stuffed from the neck end and later cooked so that the head retains its natural shape (which is much easier said than done, I might add).

4. For the stuffing, using a meat grinder, grind the head meat, shoulder meat, pork fat, and green onions into a large mixing bowl. Stir in the Calvados and season with the pepper, coriander, nutmeg, mace, and remaining pink salt. With your hands, vigorously stir the meat mixture until everything comes together and starts to pull away from the sides of the bowl. Then add the pistachios, wild mushrooms, and the marinated tongue and heart.

5. Fill the skin of the head by scooping the meat mixture into large softballs and stuffing them into the skin, being careful not to overstuff the head as the meat will need room to expand a bit as it cooks. Wrap the head in a large cloth dish towel or 4 layers of cheesecloth. With butcher's twine, tie the ends of the cloth and add a few more trusses of twine to help the head hold its shape as it cooks.

6. To cook the pâté, preheat the oven to 250°. Place a large roasting pan over high heat on a stove top and add the calves' feet, vinegar, wine, and bay leaf. Cover with water and bring to a boil. Reduce the heat to a simmer and lay in the wrapped head. Cover the pan with foil and simmer 10 minutes. Transfer the pan to the oven and slow-cook the pâté in the bouillon for about 5 hours.

7. Remove the pan from the oven and cool in the bouillon in the refrigerator overnight. To serve, unwrap the pâté from the cloth and carefully remove the butcher twine stitches. Slice the pâté, beginning from the back of the head toward the nose, slicing as thinly as possible. Serve the chilled pâté proudly with the natural gelée formed in the roasting pan along with crusty bread, mustard, and pickles.

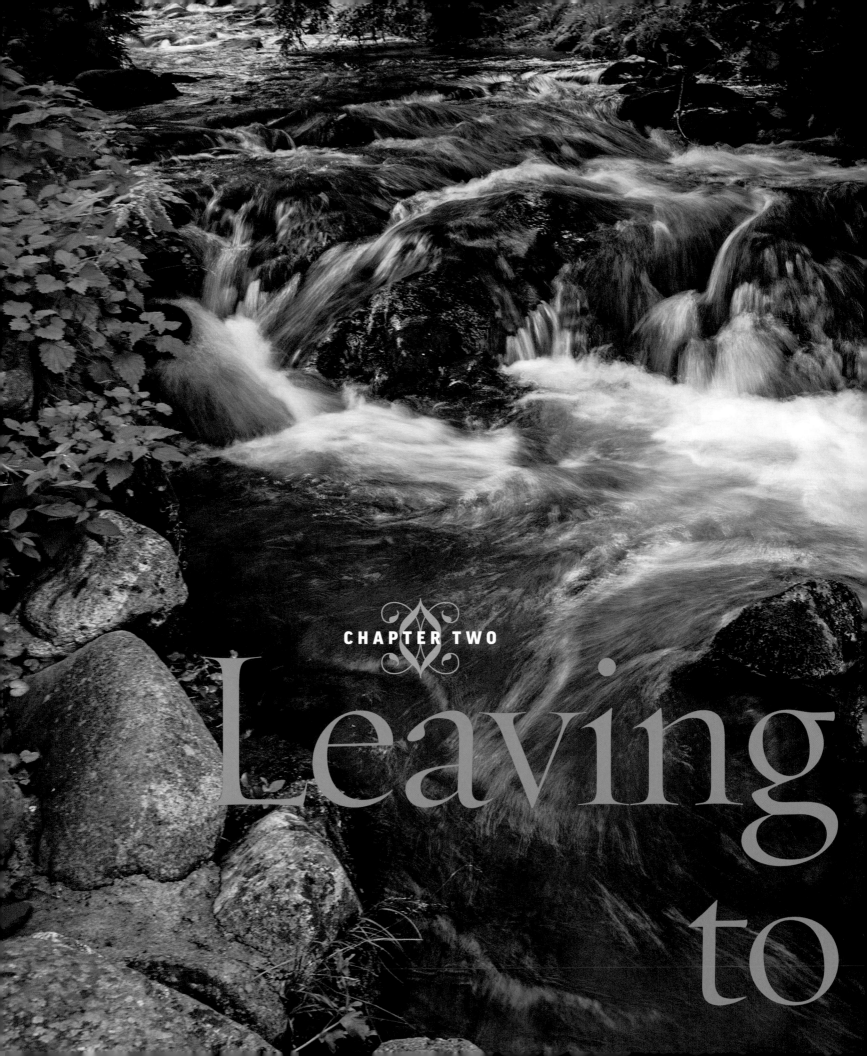

CHAPTER TWO

Leaving
to

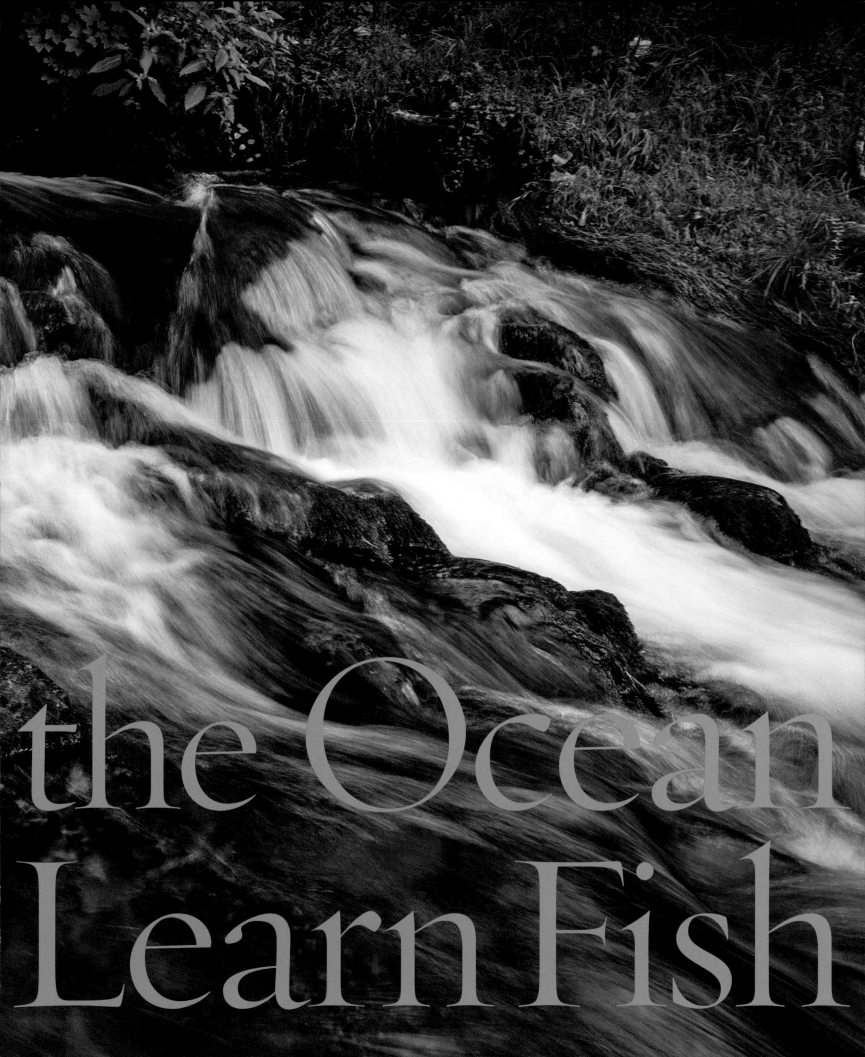

F

ISHING IS ONE THING I know. I've been doing it since I was a little kid, with everything from cane poles to fly rods, from fish traps to seine nets, and even, on occasion, with bow and arrow. High school meant boarding with the religious order of the Brothers of the Sacred Heart at St. Stanislaus High School on the Bay St. Louis. I was so well-versed in fishing that some of my best memories of that time on the Mississippi Gulf Coast were gigging for flounder at night, wading waist-deep in the warm, sandy shallows of the pristine, salty estuary that opened into the Gulf of Mexico. With spears in one hand and lanterns in the other, I would try to make out the outline of the delicious flat fish that found refuge among the crabs, jellyfish, and stingrays in the still water of flats.

BECOMING FISH STOCK, left, a head of St. Pierre peeks out from a bath of leek, onion, celery, carrot, and bay leaf. Overleaf, the beautiful babbling brook that runs through the Spielweg valley.

If I was both patient and lucky, I'd return to school with a flounder that Brother Pierre, our school chef, would fillet and fry up to be devoured with a little brown butter and parsley—essentially meunière. Since this beat the hell out of what the other students were eating, early on fishing paid off for me big time.

It's not just that I've been fishing since I was old enough to hold a pole, I've cooked fish my whole life, too. Today, we live on Bayou Liberty, just a stone's throw from the place where I caught and cooked my very first bass, sacalait, and perch. Gulf seafood was such a prominent part of my childhood that every community gathering

seemed to feature either a fish fry, a seafood gumbo cook-off, or a crab, shrimp, or crawfish boil. Even today, on any given spring Friday at any given Catholic church, you'll still find the Knights of Columbus frying up hundreds of pounds of fish. My first restaurant jobs, at age 14, were at local seafood restaurants: the Cast Net, Meyer's, and Chef Buster's, where cases upon cases of redfish, speckled trout, pompano, American reds, mangrove, and B-line snapper were delivered—filleted and skinned—always fresh, never frozen, ready for the cast iron pan or the deep-fat fryer. I wasn't a fish cook, but I did lug around the fish and mix the crab and shrimp dressings that we'd stuff into every filet. Those fish tasted

TOWARD A PERFECT TROUT, left. A local fisherman delivers wild, live fish to the Spielweg's tank where they're killed, cleaned, and in the pan in minutes.

"It's not just that I've been fishing since I was old enough to hold a pole, I've cooked fish my whole life, too. Fish was one thing I knew about. Or so I thought."

bestowing Michelin stars upon it in the 1990s, thus making it a world-class destination. Three months after I arrived as an apprentice cook I had my first chance to prove myself by cooking an actual protein—in this case a very recently living fish. I was feeling a bit trapped by my long assignment at the *entremetier* station where I handled every vegetable, pasta, potato, soup, and rice imaginable. And though everything I touched and cooked did wind up on a plate, not until that day did the sous chef consider me ready for fish.

It was a Monday, however, a day of limited service when the hotel and restaurant were closed to outside guests and we cooked only for the few who had remained in our care since the weekend. I was in the kitchen with Bertrand, our very proud and very Alsatian sous chef, a man who carried a bit of a chip on his broad shoulders, convinced that every move he made would reflect on the culinary reputation of the entire nation of France. Technically I had not moved to the fish station, though Mondays and Tuesdays did allow for a bit of cross training. Perhaps, I thought, at last he would see how my skills were being wasted on potatoes, pasta, and vegetables. Fish was my chance to impress the hard-charging Frenchman.

Suddenly, the order came in. It was read out in a mixture of French and German, carefully communicated verbally by Bertrand, who'd been handed the billet with reverence by the service staff. He looked over at me and quietly said, *"Ein Forelle müllerin."* Ha! I knew what that was: trout meunière, not only Brother Pierre's favorite thing to cook, but my Mom's, too. Here was my chance, at last, to show them how we do it back home. I could see it now, the word sweeping across the foothills of

like we wanted fish to taste: spicy, well-cooked, and delicious. So I hope you get the picture: Fish was one thing I knew about. Or so I thought.

Imagine my surprise, then, when I was honored with the opportunity to cook a fish in the kitchen of Karl-Josef Fuchs's Spielweg, the Black Forest restaurant so renowned that even the French held it in high esteem,

37

the Alps, through entire countries that have never even *heard* of Cajun spices. At last I'd be held in high esteem by great chefs on both sides of the Rhine: The name Besh would rank with the Bavarian Wolfgang Kaufmann, the German Dieter Müller, the Austrian Eckart Witzigmann, not to mention French giants like Bocuse, Vergé, and Blanc. Ready to assume my soon-to-be fame, I secretly mixed a dish of salt, black pepper, cayenne pepper, white pepper, garlic powder, onion salt, and ground celery seed. Armed with my Cajun spices, I skedaddled

to the live-fish holding tank built right into the back of the kitchen.

Each week throughout the season, fishermen would deliver their live catch from the surrounding brooks and streams. My chef and his father and his grandfather before him had generations of relationships with these fishermen and their families. There was no checking in cases of fish as we did routinely in most American restaurants. Here, the fisherman knew better than the cook what constituted an excellent *Bachforelle,* or brook trout. Nor were all of these fish pre-filleted; or for that matter, pre-dead. No. If you were to work the fish station, you would have to catch, kill, clean, and then finally cook the fish yourself. Imagine a busy night: fish in various stages of the process, sometimes literally jumping out of the poaching pot of vinegar courtbouillon where they would turn a beautiful bluish hue (what the French have called for centuries *truite au bleu,* was in Münstertal, *Forelle blau*).

Back home when we'd catch fish, we'd throw them into the ice chest, close it, and let them die, pretty much out of sight and out of mind. They might flop around a bit, but not much thought was given to their demise. Here in the Black Forest, however, Karl-Josef had a different ethic: the fish, like the game animals he hunted, would be killed swiftly and respectfully, thus preserving flavor and texture, as well as a kind of spiritual quality.

Given the order to cook the *Forelle müllerin,* it took me several attempts to scoop the live fish from the holding pool. *Forelle* in hand, but just barely, I whacked it on the head with a large wooden spoon to stun it, then pierced its head with a sharp fillet knife. Quickly I removed the entrails under cold running mountain water (saving the trimmings, of course, for fertilizer in Sabine's garden). With a tablespoon, I scraped every square centimeter of the trout, removing the last tiny scale. Then I smothered it in my Cajun spices, dredged it in flour, and fried it in a half inch of clarified butter. The fish looked beautiful in a sort of tacky way, almost chicken-fried. Its warm golden brown crust had a reddish tint, admittedly different from any trout that I'd seen in this kitchen. But I was here to make my mark on this quaint Black Forest cooking tradition. I could see it now: commercials right out of a *Saturday Night Live* sketch: "Ich bin Chef John Besh und I'm here to spice you up!"

Proud of my creation, I move forward to the pass where food from all over the kitchen was brought to be plated by the sous chef. Bertrand's first words to me were, "Where is the ketchup and the hushpuppies?" He quickly pointed out mockingly to the entire staff: What I'd

> *"I scraped every square centimeter of the trout. Then I smothered it in Cajun spices and fried it in clarified butter. It looked beautiful in a sort of tacky way."*

cooked was quintessentially American, with no regard whatsoever for the natural flavor of the fish. He went on to question my ability to even *taste* my food, since we Americans were "raised on McDonald's, French fries, and ketchup on everything." I tried to explain that I wasn't really all that American, being from New Orleans, but to no avail. From that moment, I, along with the whole country of my birth, was drummed off the fish station. Sent back to potatoes and pasta. It would be many months before they let me near a trout again.

THE KITCHEN BRIGADE, left, has the same feeling as when I was there 20 years ago. Above, an old print in the dining room.

39

BROOK TROUT MÜLLERIN

Serves 2

4 skin-on brook trout filets

Salt

Freshly ground black pepper

¼ cup flour

4 tablespoons butter

1 lemon, halved

Leaves from 4 sprigs fresh parsley, chopped

TROUT COOKED THIS WAY IS CALLED *MÜLLERIN,* "the miller's wife's" fish, because it's made from filets of mountain trout fished from the stream that powers the flour mill. It is precisely the same preparation and derivation as the French meunière. Don't be fooled by its apparent simplicity: layers of flavor are built by each ingredient in its turn—it is elegant in its simplicity. The trout filets are lightly coated with flour, browned in a pan with good butter, and by the time the fish is cooked, the butter has turned nutty brown and the fish is crisp and tender. Just before serving, a squeeze of lemon and freshly chopped parsley turn the butter in the pan into bubbly foam which is then spooned over each filet.

1. Season both sides of the filets with salt and pepper and lightly dust with flour. Melt the butter in a large skillet over medium-high heat. Place the filets, skin-side down, and cook until the skin is brown and crispy, 3–5 minutes. Carefully turn with a spatula and cook for another 30 seconds.

2. Squeeze the lemon over the fish and add the parsley. As the sauce begins to bubble up, spoon ample butter over each filet and serve immediately.

BASIC FISH STOCK

Makes about 5 cups

3 pounds fish heads and bones

1 small onion, chopped

1 leek, rinsed and chopped

1 stalk celery, chopped

1 carrot, peeled and chopped

1 clove garlic, crushed

½ cup dry white wine

1 bay leaf

1 sprig fresh tarragon

1 sprig fresh thyme

THERE ARE TWO EXCELLENT REASONS for making fish stock. First, it ensures that no part of the fish goes to waste; and second, you can use the flavorful stock to coax flavor from pan sauces and soups. I like to use more delicately flavored fish of the white-fleshed variety when making stock. I find the subtle flavors result in a lovely sauce with no fishy undertones. We use this stock in Sautéed St. Pierre (page 53) and other fish dishes.

1. Put the fish heads and bones in a large heavy-bottomed pot with the onions, leeks, celery, carrots, garlic, and wine along with the bay leaf, tarragon, and thyme. Cover with 8 cups water and bring to a boil over high heat. Reduce the heat and simmer, uncovered, for 1 hour. Strain through a fine mesh strainer. Press all the goodness from the fish and discard the solids. You can cool and freeze the stock or use it immediately.

FORELLE BLAU: TRUITE AU BLEU

Serves 4

½ cup white vinegar

Salt

4 very fresh whole trout, scaled and gutted

6 tablespoons butter

Leaves from 4 sprigs fresh parsley, chopped

1 lemon, quartered

I FIRST ENCOUNTERED THE ICONIC BLUE TROUT in the pages of M. F. K. Fisher's early memoir, *The Gastronomical Me*, where she described a meal in an old mill in northern Burgundy. But her truite au bleu was a remote image of something so delicate it could only be experienced under the perfect circumstances, none of which had happened for me until I went to the Black Forest. There, where *Forelle blau* has been a delicacy for generations, Karl-Josef has a freshwater fish tank right outside his kitchen so that he can have it on the menu almost year-round. The fish must be taken straight from the water so its mucilage can interact with the vinegar in the cooking water, turning the fish its signature color and achieving its classic curl on the plate. Search out the freshest trout for this dish, but unless it's so fresh that the fish is still slimy, you won't have as bright a color, but you'll still have the flavor.

1. Add the vinegar to a large pot of salted water and bring to a boil. Put the trout in the pot and simmer for 5 minutes. The trout will turn blue and begin to curl. Don't worry if the skin breaks in the pot. Carefully transfer fish directly to a plate with a spider or two slotted spoons.

2. Meanwhile, melt the butter in a small skillet over medium heat, then cook until it turns golden brown, swirling the pan occasionally, 4–5 minutes. Drizzle the browned butter over the trout, sprinkle with the parsley, and serve with fresh lemon.

1. The fresh trout emerges from a large pot of vinegary water showing its signature blue color.

2. Directly from the pot, the blue trout awaits browned butter, parsley, and lemon juice.

43

WHY FAMILY MEAL MATTERS

In Order to Cook Well, Chefs Have to Eat Well, Too

TOO OFTEN IN A COOK'S DAY mealtimes happen either too early or too late, taken in the off hours before a lunch or dinner shift. We call these "family meals," and their quality ranges from merely acceptable to utterly abysmal. Of course in a restaurant kitchen there are never enough cooks to do what needs to be done. So the American mode at family meal has become to lower our heads and shovel down the food in a fashion more common to livestock. After all, a cook has a station to prep, and within the hour real meals to cook for paying guests. But I have always judged a cook by the quality of his or her contributions to family meal. Obviously, the choicest ingredients aren't used, so it takes a little thought and a lot of heart to turn out a memorable meal for the staff (like the Spielweg's above).

Nor does this stop just at our borders. It's not as if our European comrades are being raised on farm fresh milk just moments from the barn, or that breakfast means fresh croissants every morning with the most beautiful fresh-churned butter. In a world that's become proficient at turning out pretty good cooks at breakneck speed, insidiously, we're turning out poor eaters as well.

The family meal at the Spielweg was genius! The Fuchs family would sit down each day before lunch and dinner service with the entire staff of the restaurant. While the family usually dined at their centuries-old family table, the *Stammtisch*, we enjoyed ours at two large tables, set beautifully, very often with flowers and occasionally with wine. Often, we'd drink a *Schorle*, a goblet of whatever fruit juice was in season combined with sparkling water made in the cellar. Our meals were lavish by today's standards: each station in the kitchen was required to prepare a contribution. Vegetables, starches, and soups from the *entremetier*—our sous chef would assign us an ingredient to cook with—potatoes, apples, kale, turnips, dandelion greens. Dessert came from the patisserie; the baker turned out lovingly hand-crafted loaves. The *garde manger* would create a salad or a cold appetizer. Meats and fish all came from the saucier.

The Fuchs family had a regular regimen based on certain Badischer traditions (meaning they came from the Baden region of Southern Germany). As a New Orleans native I could certainly appreciate them since I was reared on such traditions as red beans and rice every Monday of my childhood. At the Spielweg we enjoyed *Ochsenfleisch mit Bouillonkartoffeln* (boiled beef with potatoes in broth) on Saturday. Friday was always fish. And Sunday was delicate schnitzel of turkey or pork that I still can taste today.

Even though we Americans have made progress producing great cooks in large numbers through many excellent culinary education programs, these so-called well-trained cooks are often disasters at family meal. They're not given much instruction on eating in a civilized manner: taking the time to sit down and enjoy not just the food but the company of others at the table, too. Believe it or not, even some of my own cooks live on wretched snacks of frozen pizza, fast food burgers, and bagged chips. When they think salad, they think gloppy dressing; when they think drink, they think sweet, syrupy sodas; and when they think breakfast, they think cold, artificially flavored processed cereal drowning in milk as thin as water.

While it is impractical and probably unaffordable to have Spielweg-style family meals in most American restaurants, I do believe that in order to cook well we must learn, as cooks, to eat well, too. Since we have drifted precariously far from our own family tables, where these lessons have been passed down since the beginning of time, those Spielweg family meals gave me an enlightened perspective. They taught me to at least encourage my own cooks to enjoy family meals prepared and served in the same spirit.

POACHED ARCTIC CHAR

Serves 6

1 whole fennel bulb
   with stalks, sliced

4 small carrots

2 stalks celery,
   roughly chopped

4 sprigs fresh thyme

1 lemon, sliced

1 bay leaf

1 teaspoon whole
   coriander

1 teaspoon mustard
   seeds

   Generous pinch
   red pepper flakes

2 cups white wine

   Salt

   Freshly ground
   black pepper

1 4-pound whole
   arctic char, scaled
   and gutted

   Fennel Choucroute
   (page 48)

THERE IS SUCH AN ELEGANCE to the well-presented, perfectly poached whole fish. This char has a luxurious texture that's perfectly balanced with the brininess of a slow-cooked Fennel Choucroute. I serve this dish with a kind of ceremony. By that I mean the fish poacher itself becomes part of the act. We gather around just waiting for the reveal—the moment the fish is lifted from the liquid and onto a platter. The aromatics fill the room as the steaming fish is set in the place of honor at the table.

1. In a fish poacher or large roasting pan, combine the fennel, carrots, celery, thyme, lemon, bay leaf, coriander, mustard seeds, and pepper flakes; cover with the wine and 2 cups cold water. Bring to a boil over high heat, then reduce the heat to a bare simmer. Season with salt and pepper. Slide the fish into the poaching liquid, cover with a lid or foil, and poach 20–25 minutes, until cooked through.

2. To serve, gently lift the fish from the poacher and onto a large platter. Serve with the Fennel Choucroute.

FENNEL CHOUCROUTE

Serves 6

5 tablespoons
olive oil

2 fennel bulbs,
thinly sliced

2 leeks, white and
light green parts,
thinly sliced
lengthwise

1 large onion,
thinly sliced

3 cloves garlic,
thinly sliced

½ cup rice vinegar

2 cups white wine

2 teaspoons sugar

2 teaspoons caraway
seeds

Salt

Freshly ground
black pepper

LONG, THIN SLICES OF FENNEL AND LEEK make all the difference in creating a texture that mimics traditional cabbage choucroute. The sweet and sour flavors are a perfect balance to fish like Poached Arctic Char (page 47). The fennel's mild anise flavor heightened by caraway seeds works brilliantly with the slightly oily texture of the fish. Choucroute is wonderful, too, with sausages, pork, and duck.

1. Heat the oil in a large heavy-bottomed pot over medium heat. Add the fennel, leeks, onions, and garlic and cook until they are soft and translucent, about 10 minutes. Add the vinegar, white wine, sugar, and caraway and bring to a boil, stirring occasionally. Season with salt and pepper.

2. Reduce the heat to low, cover, and cook, stirring occasionally, until the vegetables are opaque and tender, about 20 minutes.

BASIC SHRIMP STOCK

Makes about 6 cups

3 tablespoons
   olive oil

3 pounds wild
   Gulf shrimp heads
   and shells

1 small onion,
   chopped

1 leek, chopped

1 stalk celery,
   chopped

2 bay leaves

1 teaspoon black
   peppercorns

BELIEVE IT OR NOT, there is more flavor in shrimp heads and shells than there is in the shrimp meat itself. Shrimp stock is an intensely flavored base that I love to use for many of my soups, stews, and sauces. In Louisiana, shrimp stock is essential to the traditional étouffées that I grew up with. I was surprised to discover that it is equally as common in Provence. There they use a combination of any and all shellfish: crab, shrimp, langoustines, *écrivisses*, lobsters. You can, too.

1. Heat the oil in a large heavy-bottomed pot over high heat. Add the shrimp heads and shells and toast the shells, stirring occasionally, for about 10 minutes. Add the onions, leeks, and celery and cook until tender, about 3 minutes. Cover the shells with 8 cups water, add the bay leaves and peppercorns, and bring to a boil.

2. Reduce the heat to low and simmer, uncovered, for about 2 hours. Strain through a fine mesh strainer. Press all the goodness from the shells, then discard them. You can cool and freeze the stock or use it immediately.

49

LOUP DE MER POACHED IN SHRIMP BROTH

Serves 4

2 tablespoons olive oil

1 shallot, chopped

1 clove garlic, finely chopped

3-4 cups Basic Shrimp Stock (page 49)

Juice of 1 lemon

Pinch saffron

Pinch crushed red pepper flakes

Salt

Freshly ground black pepper

4 filets loup de mer or sea bass, skin scored

1 pound wild Gulf shrimp, peeled and deveined

4 tablespoons butter

Leaves from 2 sprigs fresh basil

LOUP DE MER IS THE SEA BASS also known as branzino. Slowly poached and served in an aromatic stock, nearly any fish filet will love this treatment.

1. Heat the oil in a medium skillet over medium heat. Add the shallots and garlic and cook until the shallots are tender, about 4 minutes. Add the Shrimp Stock, lemon juice, saffron, and pepper flakes and bring to a simmer. Season with salt and pepper.

2. Sprinkle both sides of the filets with salt and add to the skillet in a single layer. If the filets are not submerged, add a bit more stock. Poach the fish at a low simmer for 3 minutes, then add the shrimp. Continue poaching until the shrimp are pink and opaque, just 2 or 3 minutes more. Gently transfer the fish and shrimp to shallow soup bowls.

3. To finish the stock, raise the heat to high and bring to a boil, then stir in the butter. Ladle the stock over the fish and shrimp and sprinkle with the basil.

MARINATED SALMON WITH DILL & MUSTARD SAUCE

Serves 6

1 2–3-pound salmon filet

Heaping ¼ cup kosher salt

1 tablespoon crushed coriander

½ teaspoon ground white pepper

2 tablespoons sugar

¼ cup Dijon mustard

1 tablespoon sugar

1 tablespoon canola oil

Leaves from 8 sprigs fresh dill, chopped

Salt

Freshly ground black pepper

THIS SPICE-CURED SALMON is perfect for hors d'oeuvres or as a first course. If you're serving more people, buy a larger filet.

1. To cure the salmon, dry the filet with paper towels and place on a large platter. Sprinkle the flesh with the salt, coriander, pepper, and sugar. Cover with plastic wrap and refrigerate overnight. Rinse the salmon, pat dry, and return to the platter. Refrigerate, uncovered, overnight.

2. To make the sauce, whisk together the mustard, sugar, and oil in a small bowl. Fold in the dill and season with salt and pepper.

3. To serve the salmon, slice very thinly and serve with the mustard sauce.

SAUTÉED ST. PIERRE WITH CRAB & TWO CELERIES

Serves 4

1 Yukon Gold or yellow potato, peeled and roughly chopped

1 celery root, peeled and roughly chopped

Salt

4 tablespoons butter

Freshly ground black pepper

4 filets St. Pierre or sole

¼ cup Wondra flour

2 tablespoons canola oil

½ cup Basic Fish Stock (page 40)

Zest and juice of 1 lemon

4 ounces lump crabmeat

Leaves from 1 celery heart

1 tablespoon olive oil

THIS DISH MAY SEEM MORE COMPLEX than it really is. Feel free to make the purée well in advance and reheat it just before serving. The celery and lemon have a way of elevating any delicate fish filet such as St. Pierre (aka John Dory). These fish might be a challenge to find; sole is a perfect substitute.

1. Put the potato and celery root in a medium pot and cover with about an inch of cold water and 1 teaspoon salt. Bring to a boil and simmer until the potato is tender, 20–25 minutes; drain. Purée with 2 tablespoons of the butter in a food processor. Season with salt and pepper. Keep warm.

2. Meanwhile, season the fish with salt and pepper and dust both sides with the flour. Heat the oil in a large skillet over medium-high heat. Add the filets and cook until both sides are golden brown and the fish is flaky, 5–7 minutes on each side. Remove the fish from the pan.

3. Make the sauce by adding the Fish Stock, lemon juice, and remaining 2 tablespoons butter to the skillet. Cook over medium-high heat until the butter is melted and the liquid is slightly reduced, about 5 minutes.

4. Meanwhile, in a small bowl, toss the crabmeat with the celery leaves, olive oil, and lemon zest.

5. To serve, spoon some purée on each plate, lay a filet on top, then spoon the sauce over the fish and top with crab and celery salad.

SARDINES IN ESCABECHE

Serves 6

6 whole sardines,
   scaled and gutted

   Salt

   Freshly ground
   black pepper

   Olive oil

1 red onion, thinly
   sliced

2 carrots, peeled and
   thinly sliced

2 small red and
   yellow bell
   peppers, sliced

2 green onions,
   chopped

3 cloves garlic, finely
   chopped

¼ cup white wine
   vinegar

1 teaspoon sugar

   A few pinches
   piment d'Espelette
   or crushed red
   pepper flakes

IN ANCIENT TIMES, there were no borders between France and Spain: people ate the same food and prepared it in much the same way. The Spanish *escabeche* meant a way to preserve food all around the Mediterranean; it still does today. *Escabeche* is simply a dish of half-cooked fish that finishes "cooking" in a warm, vinegary marinade. Fresh sardines are sometimes difficult to find, but fresh mackerel or bluefish are fine substitutes. I serve this dish as a lovely appetizer right from the dish I use to marinate the fish. It's beautiful.

1. Season both sides of the sardines with salt and pepper. Heat 2 tablespoons olive oil in a large skillet over medium-high heat. In batches, sear the sardines on both sides until the skins are crisped, 2–3 minutes. Transfer to a serving dish.

2. In the same skillet, add more olive oil, along with the red onions, carrots, bell peppers, green onions, garlic, vinegar, sugar, and *piment d'Espelette*. Bring to a boil and simmer for 2 minutes. You're making a warm, sweet, and sour vinaigrette— *escabeche*. Pour the sauce over the sardines, cover with plastic wrap, and marinate for at least an hour or overnight in the refrigerator. Serve right from the dish with crusty bread.

1. Lay the cleaned squid body on a cutting board, press down to hold it in place, and slice it in half horizontally with a chef's knife.

2. Fold the two slices of squid body lengthwise into a long roll and cut into thin, spaghetti-like rings.

3. Mix the cooked spaghetti and squid together; toss with basil, lemon juice; grate bottarga over the top.

SQUID WITH SPAGHETTI & BOTTARGA

Serves 4

1 pound dried spaghetti

⅓ cup olive oil

4 cloves garlic, thinly sliced

A few pinches red pepper flakes

1 pound large squid, thinly sliced

1 pint cherry tomatoes, halved

Leaves from 4 sprigs fresh basil, roughly chopped

Zest and juice of 1 lemon

Salt

Freshly ground black pepper

Bottarga

Grated Parmesan cheese

THIS IS THE PERFECT LAST MINUTE DINNER, when I remember to go by the fish store for some fresh squid. By all means clean the squid yourself. Not only is it cheaper, it's fun to do. I like to grate *bottarga,* dried tuna or mullet roe, over the top of the pasta.

1. Cook the spaghetti in a large pot of boiling, salted water until al dente, about 10 minutes. Drain.

2. Heat the oil in a large skillet over medium-high heat. Add the garlic and pepper flakes and cook about 2 minutes. Add the squid and tomatoes and cook for just

another minute. Don't overcook the squid or it will become rubbery.

3. Add the drained pasta and the water clinging to it, the basil, lemon zest and juice to the squid in the skillet and toss well. Season with salt and pepper. Grate *bottarga* over the pasta, and toss with Parmesan.

ROASTED SEA BASS PROVENÇAL

Serves 4

1 large (3–4-pound) whole sea bass, scaled and gutted

Salt

Freshly ground black pepper

4 cloves garlic, smashed

1 shallot, sliced

Generous pinch crushed red pepper flakes

4 sprigs fresh thyme

1 orange, sliced

3 tablespoons olive oil

1 small fennel bulb, chopped

1 pint cherry tomatoes, halved

2 small red and yellow bell peppers, sliced

½ cup pitted olives, black or green

1 cup white wine

4 tablespoons butter

2 green onions, chopped

Leaves from 2 sprigs fresh basil

I USE BLACK BASS OR SNAPPER IN SEASON, but any beautiful large whole white-fleshed fish will work perfectly for this roast. I love the presentation of serving the whole fish family-style right from the pan, and I especially enjoy the ceremony of spooning the fish and vegetables onto each plate with plenty of delicious pan sauce.

1. Preheat the oven to 450°. Score the fish and season inside and out with salt and pepper. Stuff with the garlic, shallot, red pepper, thyme, and orange slices. Place the fish in a roasting pan or paella pan with the olive oil and scatter the fennel, tomatoes, peppers, and olives all around. Add the wine.

2. Roast until the fish is white and flaky and the tomatoes are beautifully charred, about 20 minutes.

3. Stir the butter into the pan and toss with the tomatoes. Sprinkle the bass with green onions and basil and serve from the pan with the tomato and olive pan sauce.

1. Score the whole fish, stuff with herbs, and lay in a roasting pan with olive oil and fennel.

2. Scatter the tomato halves, peppers, garlic, and olives around the fish and roast.

GRILLED DAURADE STUFFED WITH LEMON & FENNEL

Serves 6

3 1-pound whole daurade, porgy, or other small whole fish, scaled and gutted

Olive oil

Salt

Freshly ground black pepper

2 lemons, preferably Meyer

1 fennel bulb with fronds

THERE'S NOTHING SIMPLER or more delicious than whole fish turning golden and crispy on the grill. I have a grill basket made for hamburgers that just fits three fish and makes them a snap to turn. If you have some dried fennel seeds or stalks, throw them on the coals; it'll smell like Provence.

1. Prepare a charcoal or gas grill, or heat a grill pan on high. Rub the fish with a couple of tablespoons of olive oil and season all over with salt and pepper. Slice one lemon and put some slices inside each fish. Trim the stalks from the fennel, thinly slice the bulb, and stuff the slices and some fronds into the fish.

2. If you have a grill basket, use it, but if not, lay the stuffed fish directly on the grill. Cover and grill, turning once, until the fish is cooked through, 10–15 minutes. Remove the fish from the grill and drizzle with more olive oil and a squirt of Meyer lemon juice.

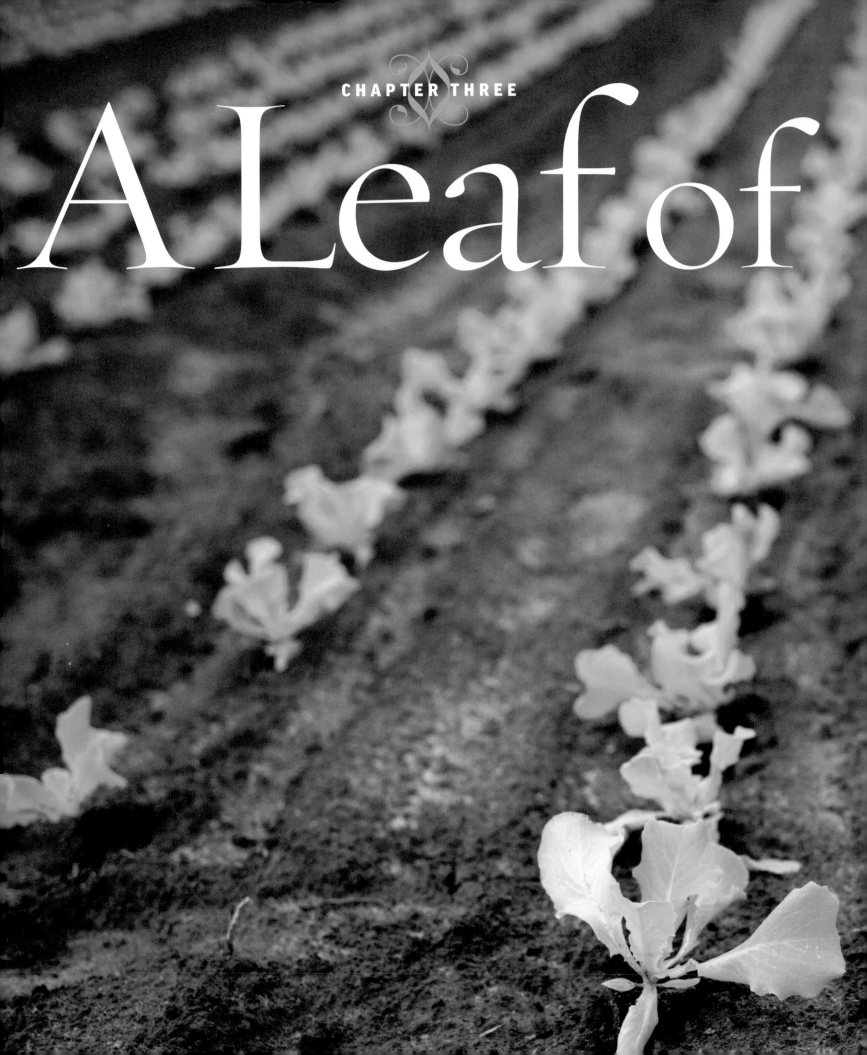

A Leaf of

Lettuce

RECIPES

B

EFORE I
arrived at the Spielweg in 1993, I had only worked
in restaurants (and some good ones at that) where
salad greens came to the door pre-packaged, pre-
washed, and stuffed into a plastic bag ready to be
opened and dressed. What that meant was until the
time I entered Karl-Josef's kitchen, I had only made
salads that tasted like dressings, not lettuces. One
day, Bertrand Lott, the French sous chef and my im-
mediate boss, assigned me to make a salad of mâche,
the small delicate green that grows in clusters and
has a sweet, subtle flavor. The Münstertal valley we
lived in was quite famous for its beekeepers; they
produced amazing varieties of honey that tasted of
the Alpine woods and wildflowers, of pear, plum,
and apple blossoms.

**IN HER SANCTUARY, left, Sabine Fuchs finds peace in the early morning
ritual of tending her lush, productive garden. Overleaf, tender lettuce
plants are cultivated in the fertile Rhine River valley near the Spielweg.**

"I quickly figured out that as the first American cook in his kitchen, I was no better than a ham-handed Bavarian and he had better hopes for me than that."

If it bloomed here, it was cultivated into honey. So I thought, why not dress that mâche salad with a honey mustard vinaigrette? I'd start with their fruit blossom honey, spike it with some ultra sharp Dijon mustard, then mix in some honey vinegar and local hazelnut oil. I thought the result was heavenly—creamy, sweet, spicy, and nutty. And I considered myself years ahead. I mean, honey mustard is a no-brainer. Even McDonald's had the stuff back then. I thought it was my duty to prove just how savvy we American chefs are: I'd dress those tender little mâche leaves with my glossy, rich dressing and everyone would surely recognize my culinary brilliance.

I served this salad one afternoon to the kitchen and dining room staff for family meal. The moment was all mine. I looked around the table and saw cooks and servers enjoying or at least eating my salad. But they uttered not a word about its distinguished gastronomical merits. They just went on eating. Until my barn-door-sized chef, with a disgusted look on his round and otherwise happy-go-lucky face, planted himself right across the table from where I sat. Looking down on me from his over-six-foot-height, Karl-Josef Fuchs himself began to yell at me in at least three languages.

His anger was extremely off-putting because I had never heard him even raise his voice before and because of his rapid combination of German, French, and English, I didn't know what the hell he was saying. But I needed no translation to understand the implication. Why, why, why would I ever do that to a leaf of lettuce?

He hated my dressing and he hated the fact that I would even consider bringing the idea of a sweet honey mustard dressing into his house. I did understand that in Baden-Württemberg, where he lives, people respect their food and don't appreciate foolish cooking like those in Bayern, which is to say in Bavaria. If I wanted honey mustard, he continued, I should go to Munich. Here, he was saying, we are more subtle and truer to the flavor of our ingredients. Evidently I had touched a delicate cultural nerve that really resonated with him. Shocked by his response to what I'd believed to be a delicious salad dressing, I quickly figured out that as the first American cook in his kitchen, I was no better than a ham-handed Bavarian and he had better hopes for me than that. Not knowing just how badly Bavarians cook, I really didn't know what to think, although I surely knew I'd never make a sweet honey mustard dressing again.

Later, after our midday family meal and a chance to cool off, Karl-Josef took me aside. He had me taste every kind of lettuce, each leaf of which had been carefully raised from seed in Sabine's kitchen garden, then gently and individually washed in the kitchen. This was the first time I truly discerned the subtle flavor distinctions of each leaf. I got Karl-Josef's point and realized that those delicate flavors had to be differentiated and celebrated. That they must be paired with just the right oils and vinegars to enhance and balance their natural qualities, never to drown them. And this was how I learned to prepare a salad in a restaurant using individual organic leaves that had been grown and picked by someone who cares. This was the first time I understood that my goal was not to manipulate that leaf of lettuce, but to respect it. It's amazing how so many blunders have taught me my biggest food (and life) lessons ever.

66

AS MASTER OF the hotel and restaurant, Sabine dresses in the traditonal dirndl of Southern Germany, below right with Zorro. With Josefine Fuchs, Karl-Josef's mother, below. The spa is tucked into a garden cottage, above. A stalk of borage in bloom, far left.

MÂCHE SALAD WITH PUMPKIN OIL VINAIGRETTE

Serves 6

4 slices thick bacon, cut into lardons

4 slices country bread, roughly cubed

Salt

½ shallot, finely chopped

3 tablespoons sherry vinegar

2 tablespoons canola oil

2 teaspoons pumpkin seed oil

Freshly ground black pepper

8 handfuls mâche

MOST SALAD DRESSINGS are made in advance and kept in the refrigerator. But mâche is such a delicate leaf that I never want to drown it in a heavy pre-made dressing. So I mix this vinaigrette just moments before I serve the salad and use it sparingly.

1. Cook the bacon in a large skillet over medium heat until crispy. Remove and drain on paper towels. Scatter the bread cubes in the same skillet and toss to evenly coat with the bacon fat. Cook until the croutons are crunchy and golden, about 5 minutes. Sprinkle with salt and drain on paper towels. Return to the pan to crisp.

2. For the vinaigrette, whisk together the shallot, vinegar, and oils in a small bowl. Season with salt and pepper.

3. Put the mâche in a large salad bowl, drizzle with the vinaigrette, and toss gently. Sprinkle with the bacon pieces and croutons and serve.

68

JENIFER'S CUCUMBER & TOMATO SALAD

Serves 6

1 clove garlic, finely chopped

2 tablespoons red wine vinegar

2 tablespoons olive oil

Salt

Freshly ground black pepper

4 Persian cucumbers, peeled and cubed

1 pint cherry tomatoes of different colors, halved

½ small red onion, diced

Leaves from 2 sprigs fresh basil

Leaves from 2 sprigs fresh parsley

Leaves from 2 sprigs fresh thyme

Pinch red pepper flakes

JENIFER SAYS she could eat this salad—equal parts cubed small cucumbers and tiny cherry tomatoes—every day. You'll likely find it in our fridge throughout the summer, prized as a relish, with sandwiches, or on its own.

1. For the vinaigrette, whisk together the garlic, vinegar, and oil; season with salt and black pepper. Combine the cucumbers, tomatoes, onion, basil, parsley, and thyme in a large bowl. Season with salt, black pepper, and a pinch of red pepper. Stir in the vinaigrette and let the flavors marinate for 30 minutes before serving.

ROASTED BRUSSELS SPROUT SALAD

Serves 6

1½ pounds Brussels
   sprouts, trimmed
   and halved

   Olive oil

   Salt

   Freshly ground
   black pepper

2 cloves garlic, sliced

2 tablespoons sherry
   vinegar

2 tablespoons
   sesame oil

2 tablespoons
   hazelnut oil

THIS IS GREAT AS A FIRST COURSE but can be enjoyed as a side dish as well. Often I prepare cauliflower and/or carrots the same way. The idea is to toss the fresh-roasted vegetables while still warm with a fragrant vinaigrette. I like to serve it either hot or cold.

1. Preheat the oven to 450°. On a baking pan, toss the Brussels sprouts with a generous amount of olive oil and season with salt and pepper. Roast for about 20 minutes, until the sprouts are golden brown and tender, tossing occasionally. Transfer to a large bowl and, while the sprouts are still hot, add the garlic, vinegar, and oils. Toss, sprinkle with more salt and pepper, and serve.

LEAFY HERB SALAD WITH ROASTED NUTS

Serves 6

½ cup balsamic
  vinegar

1 tablespoon honey

3 tablespoons
  olive oil

  Salt

  Freshly ground
  black pepper

1 egg white

1 tablespoon sugar

2 pinches cayenne
  pepper

½ cup unsalted
  pistachios

¼ cup pine nuts

¼ cup roasted and
  salted pumpkin
  seeds

6 handfuls sweet
  spring greens, such
  as arugula, beet,
  or turnip

2 handfuls delicate
  herb leaves such
  as coriander, basil,
  or mint

I EAGERLY AWAIT THE FIRST tiny greens of the season to make this mixed green salad, enhanced with the crunchiness of roasted nuts.

1. Preheat the oven to 325°. Line a baking pan with parchment paper.

2. For the vinaigrette, heat the vinegar in a small skillet over low heat and simmer until it is syrupy and reduced by half, to about ¼ cup. Remove from the heat and cool slightly. Whisk in the honey and olive oil and season with salt and pepper.

3. Beat the egg white in a medium bowl until frothy and white. Whisk in the sugar, cayenne pepper, ½ teaspoon salt, and pinch black pepper. Add the pistachios, pine nuts, and pumpkin seeds and stir to coat the nuts with the egg white mixture. Spread the mixture thinly on the prepared baking pan and bake, stirring once, until golden, about 20 minutes. The nuts will be soft when they come out of the oven, but they'll become crunchy as they cool.

4. In a large bowl, combine the greens and herbs. Drizzle with the balsamic vinaigrette (a little goes a long way here) and sprinkle with the roasted nuts.

RADIANT SALADS, from left, bowls of Butter Lettuce with Creamy Herb Dressing, Carrot & Chive Salad, Roasted Beets in Vinaigrette, and Dill-Marinated Cucumbers.

BUTTER LETTUCE SALAD WITH CREAMY HERB DRESSING

Serves 6

1 cup buttermilk

¼ cup mayonnaise

¼ cup plain yogurt

2 tablespoons lemon juice

½ small bunch fresh chives, chopped

Leaves from 2 sprigs fresh dill, chopped

1 clove garlic, finely chopped

Salt

Pinch ground white pepper

1 head red leaf lettuce

1 head green leaf lettuce

THIS IS MY VERSION of the working bistro salad, the classic hors d'oeuvres variés made up of composed salads such as Carrot & Chive Salad, Roasted Beets with Vinaigrette, and Dill-Marinated Cucumbers. Often, simple sliced tomatoes with a vinaigrette sauce and boiled potatoes dressed with oil are added.

1. In a small mixing bowl, whisk together the buttermilk, mayonnaise, yogurt, lemon juice, chives, dill, and garlic. Season with salt and pepper.

2. Tear the lettuces into small pieces and pile into a large bowl. Toss the lettuces with just enough dressing to lightly coat the leaves.

CARROT & CHIVE SALAD

Serves 6

4 carrots, peeled and cut into strips

2 tablespoons rice wine vinegar

1 teaspoon canola oil

½ teaspoon toasted caraway seeds

Pinch sugar

Salt

1 tablespoon chopped fresh chives

THIS IS A VERY SIMPLE SLAW in which cabbage, fennel, or celery root can be used instead of the carrots. I cook the carrots just enough to soften them so they'll absorb the vinaigrette yet still retain their color, flavor, and crispness.

1. Bring a small pot of salted water to a boil. Add the carrots and blanch until softened but still crunchy, about 30 seconds. Drain, rinse under cold running water, and transfer to a serving bowl.

2. Whisk together the vinegar, oil, caraway, and a pinch of sugar in a small mixing bowl. Add to the carrots, season with salt, and toss. Marinate the carrots at least 30 minutes. Sprinkle with the chives before serving.

ROASTED BEETS IN VINAIGRETTE

Serves 6

4 medium beets

Olive oil

Salt

Freshly ground black pepper

3 tablespoons rice wine vinegar

2 teaspoons canola oil

Pinch sugar

1 clove garlic, thinly sliced

I LOVE TO USE BEETS in a variety of colors to make this salad more interesting, and I roast them to bring out their sweetness.

1. Preheat the oven to 400°. Wash the beets and rub with olive oil, salt, and pepper. Place on a baking pan and roast, about 1 hour or until tender.

2. When the beets are cool enough to handle, peel with a small knife or rub with paper towels to remove the skin. Cut each into 8 pieces.

3. Whisk together the vinegar, canola oil, sugar, and garlic in a medium mixing bowl. Add the beets and marinate for at least 30 minutes before serving.

DILL-MARINATED CUCUMBERS

Serves 6

2 cucumbers

2 tablespoons rice wine vinegar

1 tablespoon plain yogurt

Pinch sugar

Salt

Leaves from 1 sprig fresh dill, chopped

USE WHATEVER CUCUMBERS you have on hand and treat them to a brief marinade of dill vinegar and yogurt.

1. Peel and seed the cucumbers. Slice crosswise into small arcs and transfer to a medium bowl. Add the vinegar, yogurt, and sugar. Season with salt, stir in the dill, and mix gently. Marinate the cucumbers at least 30 minutes, then drain before serving.

GRILLED ENDIVE & RADICCHIO SALAD WITH BLACKBERRY VINAIGRETTE

Serves 6

6 tablespoons hazelnut oil

3 tablespoons sherry vinegar

1 tablespoon sugar

1½ cups blackberries

Salt

Freshly ground black pepper

2 heads radicchio

6 heads Belgian endive, halved

½ small bunch fresh chives, roughly chopped

I LOVE GRILLING THE BITTER LEAVES of endive and radicchio with a fruity vinaigrette because in the process they will lose some of their astringency and pick up a sweetness from the berries. This salad is perfect served alongside hearty grilled meats.

1. To make the vinaigrette, whisk together the hazelnut oil, vinegar, sugar, and blackberries in a large bowl. Season with salt and pepper.

2. Prepare a charcoal or gas grill or heat a grill pan on high heat. Pull off and discard the browned, outer leaves of the radicchio (leaving the root intact) and cut in quarters. Toss the endive and radicchio quickly

in the bowl with the vinaigrette and season with salt and pepper. Place the radicchio and endive directly on the grill, and cook until the pieces are charred on all sides, 3–4 minutes.

3. Remove the endive and radicchio to a platter. Spoon over the vinaigrette and the blackberries and scatter the chopped chives on top.

DANDELION GREENS & ARUGULA WITH WALNUT OIL VINAIGRETTE

Serves 6

½ shallot, finely chopped

¼ cup sherry vinegar

3 tablespoons walnut oil

1 tablespoon canola oil

1 tablespoon honey

Salt

Freshly ground black pepper

1 bunch arugula, stemmed and washed

A handful young dandelion greens

EACH SPRING I LOOK FORWARD TO the first delicate little dandelion greens and tiny arugula. The greens' peppery bite is perfectly balanced with honey and the nuttiness of walnut oil.

1. In a large salad bowl, whisk together the shallot, vinegar, oils, and honey. Season with salt and pepper. Add the greens and toss with the dressing.

WARM GOAT CHEESE SALAD WITH CHRIS'S GARLIC & ANCHOVY DRESSING

Serves 6–8

FOR THE TOASTS

4 ounces goat cheese

1 green onion, thinly sliced

1 clove garlic, minced

Leaves from 1 sprig fresh rosemary, chopped

Salt

Freshly ground black pepper

½ baguette or country bread, sliced and toasted

Red pepper flakes

Olive oil

FOR THE DRESSING

5 cloves garlic, sliced

4 filets anchovies, chopped

2 teaspoons Dijon mustard

Juice from 2 lemons

½ cup olive oil

FOR THE SALAD

2 large ripe tomatoes, sliced

1 pint cherry tomatoes, halved

1 head red leaf lettuce, leaves torn

¼ cup toasted pine nuts

YOU SEE THIS SALAD ON THE MENU of every little Provençal restaurant: Goat cheese spread on toasted croutons with lettuce, tomatoes, and a wonderfully strong and mustardy anchovy dressing. Chef Chris would make his favorite dressing with a mortar and pestle. It is lusciously creamy, yet sharpened with garlic. I love it because it reminds me of a Caesar dressing without all that Parmesan. Creamy goat cheese, tomatoes, lettuces: it's Provence in a bowl.

1. For the toasts, preheat the oven to 350°. In a small bowl, mix together the goat cheese, green onions, garlic, and rosemary; season with salt and pepper. Spread the cheese mixture on the toasts, sprinkle with red pepper flakes, and drizzle with olive oil. Heat in the oven for 5 minutes.

2. Meanwhile, make the dressing. Combine the garlic and anchovies in a mortar and pound into a paste. Add the mustard and lemon juice and pound again until the mixture comes together. Add the olive oil, a few drops at a time, mixing with the pestle between each addition. Whisk in the remaining oil until the dressing is smooth and creamy.

3. To make the salad, in a large bowl, season the tomatoes with salt and pepper. Top with the lettuce, drizzle with the garlic dressing, and sprinkle with the toasted pine nuts. Serve with goat cheese toasts.

FRIED KALE SALAD

Serves 6

Canola oil

1 bunch lacinato or Tuscan kale, stems and ribs removed

Salt

1 lemon, zested and juiced

Parmesan cheese

THIS IS HARDLY A TRADITIONAL SALAD—what I'm doing is frying kale leaves in oil which for me makes a more satisfying dish than raw kale leaves. Shavings of Parmesan lend a salty tang to every bite.

1. Heat 3 inches of oil in a medium heavy-bottomed pot to 350° on a candy thermometer. Fry the kale in batches until the edges of each leaf curl up, 1–2 minutes. Drain on paper towels and sprinkle with salt. In a large bowl, toss the fried kale with the lemon zest and juice, then top with shavings of Parmesan cheese.

OAK LEAF LETTUCE SALAD WITH FIGS & HAM

Serves 6

½ shallot, finely chopped

3 tablespoons sherry vinegar

2 tablespoons hazelnut oil

1 tablespoon canola oil

1 teaspoon honey

Salt

Freshly ground black pepper

8 handfuls oak leaf or butter lettuce

4 ounces thinly sliced country ham or prosciutto

10 figs, halved

GOOD HAZELNUT OIL AND GOOD SHERRY VINEGAR make all the difference in this tender lettuce salad enhanced with sweet figs and salty ham.

1. In a small bowl, whisk together the shallot, sherry vinegar, oils, and honey. Season with salt and pepper. Just before serving, put the lettuce in a large bowl and gently toss with the vinaigrette. Scatter the ham and figs on top.

CHAPTER FOUR

Not Just

a Potato

T

HE KITCHEN
was built around a courtyard, like the back of an
old inn, which it was. Light bounced sharply off the
meticulously maintained tiles, the stainless steel
tables, and the polished brass and copper handles
that seemed to adorn everything. Strangely, because
no kitchens had windows back home, a faint mountain breeze blowing in from the slightly open window kept the air crisp and fresh, letting in as well,
the gurgling sound of the nearby stream. That air,
those sounds, soothed our souls, as each of us, about
a dozen kitchen workers, went about the tasks of
peeling, blanching, dicing, reducing, and trimming
before the first guests arrived for dinner. Not only
was the Spielweg's kitchen the cleanest I'd ever
seen, it was by far the most professional. I was the

AT THE COLORFUL daily morning market in Freiburg in the square
surrounding the Münster Cathedral, left, potatoes are a way of life.
Overleaf, the elusive potatoes emerge from the *keller,* kitchen bound.

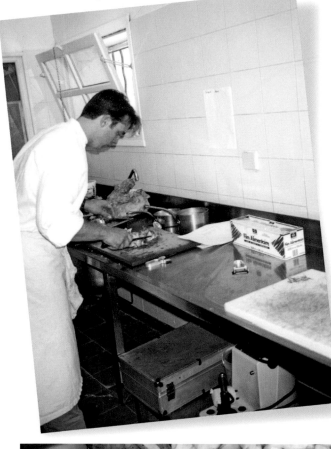

AS A YOUNG cook in 1993, above, I complete my endless prep list (and the inevitable peelings) before service. Behind the kitchen, Karl-Josef's *Käserei*, his cheesemaking room, is tucked beneath the eaves and festooned with cow bells, right.

"I was eager not only to perform some of my culinary wonders and dazzle the far-too-serious kitchen staff, but I was poised to learn, too."

cisely as a surgeon, making us always half-frightened of making a mistake. Jorg was responsible for every starch, grain, vegetable, and soup served to every guest. Which, for me, meant potatoes.

When I arrived for my first day of work at the Spielweg, in September of 1993, it was hardly my first day as a cook. I came with a certain pedigree, or so I thought. With great textbook knowledge of French cuisine, I was eager not only to perform some of my culinary wonders and dazzle what seemed to me to be a far-too-serious kitchen staff, but I was poised to learn, too. That is, if I could just recognize one single aspect of what I was supposed to do. Jorg spoke English pretty well, far better than my German. He turned out to be one of the nicest fellows I ever met and a heck of a good teacher. But on my first day at potato central, Jorg kindly created a task list for me: 1. *Kartoffelravioli*, 2. *Kartoffelmousse*, 3. *Kartoffelsoufflé*, 4. *Kartoffelgnocchi*, 5. *Schupfnudeln*, and 6. *Bouillon-Kartoffeln* for family meal. And remember to save the peelings for the pigs. Oh, and, make four liters of basic *Kartoffelsuppe,* as well as a lion's tooth butter with dandelions that we might use to perfume the soup at the last minute. I thought it nice that my chief would give his American *commis* such a list as I tried to digest the workload to be completed before service—just two hours away—and to decipher what in the world I was to cook and which recipes to follow. The recipes were written in a combination of German and French with every ingredient carefully calculated in metrics. I was now completely out of my league. Clueless.

Okay, I thought. Use some American ingenuity to tackle this one. I was a Marine, after all: First order, find the potatoes. After a futile attempt to locate any potatoes in dry storage, I began to look everywhere: the walk-in cooler, the bake shop, the cold kitchen, the cabinets in

new *commis,* just an entry-level cook. My station chief was Jorg Polke, tall and lanky, with bright blue eyes and perfectly groomed blond hair, who we somehow called "The Swede" because of his northern German heritage. To say Jorg was serious would be an understatement; he controlled his *entremetier,* or vegetable, station as pre-

"It was common for new cooks to be hazed. I was now sure I was that new guy sent searching for potatoes that didn't exist."

our main kitchen—no potatoes. Well, I thought, this has got to be some sort of a joke. Shaking off the feeling that I was annoying my new partner, I swallowed my pride and asked Jorg where I might find the potatoes. "Where else but the *keller,* of course!" So down the steep stairway to the cellar I went, finding on one side of the room thousands of dusty bottles of wine laid in catacombs at a near-perfect chilling temperature, and on the other side countless dried cured salamis and wursts, whole dry-cured hams called *Schinkenspeck,* thick slabs of bacon, and cases of staff-only beer, Fürstenberg Hefeweizen. There was lots of good stuff down there and I even contemplated stopping for a beer, but I thought better of it and ran back up to the much-too-orderly kitchen, where I swallowed hard and inquired again about the whereabouts of said *kartoffeln*. Jorg, now a bit annoyed, repeated: "the *keller!*" But this time he pointed outside, across the garden, among the barns and outbuildings, to a small half-timbered shed with a high-pitched roof. As I ran for that door, I began to think that I was being sent off on a wild goose chase (it was common for new cooks to be

hazed like that, sent scurrying off in search of a bucket of steam on a floor of a restaurant that didn't exist). I was now sure that I was that new guy, searching for potatoes in this obscure building out behind the kitchen. But to my surprise, this was no practical joke. Here, in fact and at last, was the potato *keller*.

The stone walls and floors of the *keller* kept the potatoes—unloaded from a local farmer's truck twice a season—dark, dry, and cool. As a Louisiana native, I hadn't a clue about potato season, nor had I considered how potatoes had to be stored. The potatoes in the *keller* were covered with dried soil. They needed washing badly. So I grabbed a big sack, filled it with the potatoes I'd need, and sprinted back to the kitchen, by this time covered in dirt myself. I found a sink, filled it with water and started scrubbing potatoes under running water, exposing the thin, shiny, yellow-specked flesh of each fingerling, just smaller than the palm of my hand. Next step, peel the potatoes and submerge them in clean, cold water so that they would not oxidize and turn grayish-brown. I cleaned and peeled them (being sure to save the peelings for our pigs) and submerged the peeled potatoes in a large bucket of water, just as we did in every restaurant kitchen I'd ever worked in back in the States.

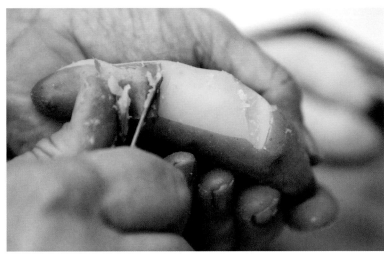

KARL-JOSEF DIRECTS his kitchen today, far left, where cooks repeat the same tasks I learned decades ago. Hand-rolled potato gnocchi, left. The yellow fingerling potato.

It was then that all hell broke loose. Our sous-chef, Bertrand, a Frenchman, stopped and called the entire kitchen around to see what I had done. Happy to be noticed, my shoulders began to straighten, my chest puffed out a bit. Not understanding a damn thing the frog was saying, I thought I was being recognized for the efficiency of my potato peeling. What was really happening was that he was chastising me for allowing the potatoes to soak in water (a practice I'd learned in cooking school). He went on to say that I had ruined the potatoes because I'd let their precious starch seep out into the water—the same starch that's crucial to producing the perfect gnocchi and *Schupfnudeln*. Without that starch, he pointed out at my expense, more flour would have to be added to the dough, and the more flour you add, the more dense the dough becomes. The more dense it becomes, the more it must be worked, and the more the dough is worked, the tougher my dough and my dumplings would be.

It was clear that I still had a lot to learn. But this became a lesson I would never forget. To this day I have recipes, like our gnocchi, that incorporate the fundamentals I learned with those fingerlings. The gnocchi recipe yields exactly one kilo of potato dough. Yet, if a cook tries to double the recipe, the result is gnocchi

that are glutinous and dense, and often grey. Because not only does the dough have to be handled too much, in the time it takes to peel twice the amount of potatoes, some inevitably discolor.

I was still to learn so much more in that kitchen in Münstertal: that good cooking takes time, patience, love, and understanding. Today I teach our young cooks that to achieve excellence you must be good at all of them. As much as I've enjoyed participating in cooking competitions, I know that speed cooking isn't really cooking. Cooking great food can only happen with adequate time to prepare. Rush it and you risk compromising quality. You need patience and that's why planning matters. It allows you to prioritize every step of the process and understand the thing you are cooking—its history as well as its chemistry. These sometimes painful lessons—learned often at my own expense (and to the amusement of my mentors)—have taught me to cook with passion and vigor. It's why I am so committed to the idea that our cooks must connect with and really understand the food at all of our restaurants. They need to know far more than where to find the potatoes (though it begins with that!). I'm proud of that rigor, and it's why the gnocchi we've served at Restaurant August, since we opened in 2001, are every bit as good as the gnocchi I learned to make, sometimes painfully, two decades ago in the Black Forest.

RÖSTI

Serves 6

3 medium Yukon
Gold or yellow
potatoes, unpeeled

Salt

Canola oil,
for frying

RÖSTI—ESSENTIALLY A LARGE PANCAKE OF GRATED POTATOES, and a traditional Swiss treasure—is quintessential mountain food. It's important to boil the potatoes in their skins to retain the starch, which helps bind the potatoes as they cook a second time in the pan. The key is to have a potato "pancake" that is perfectly browned on both sides, while still soft and tender in the center. Small, heavy, steel sauté pans are favored in restaurant kitchens, but a non-stick omelet pan will certainly do the job. I like to make the *Rösti* and hold them on a baking pan, then reheat them into a hot oven just before serving.

1. Bring the potatoes to a boil in a medium pot of cold, salted water. Reduce the heat and simmer for about 7 minutes. Drain. When the potatoes are cool enough to handle, peel with a small knife and shred on a box grater into a large bowl.

2. Cover the bottom of a small, non-stick skillet with 2 tablespoons oil and heat over medium heat. Scoop about 1 cup shredded potatoes into the skillet and gently pat down into a pancake. Fry, turning once with a large spatula, until both sides are golden and crispy, 4–6 minutes per side. Repeat to make 6 *Rösti*. Season with salt. If not serving immediately, transfer to a baking pan and pop the pan into a hot oven when you're ready to serve.

SAUTÉED POTATOES WITH QUINCE & ONIONS

Serves 6

¼ cup canola oil

4 medium yellow potatoes, peeled and diced

1 quince, peeled and diced

1 medium onion, diced

1 sprig fresh thyme

Salt

Freshly ground black pepper

JUST A SPOONFUL of these potatoes with their aromatic fruit brings a delicious balance to otherwise rich meats like pork, duck, and even hearty sausages.

1. Heat the oil in a large skillet over medium-high heat. Add the potatoes and quince and cook, stirring gently, until golden brown on all sides, 10–12 minutes.

2. Add the onions and thyme and cook, stirring frequently, until the onions are caramelized and the potatoes are tender, 8–10 minutes. Discard the thyme. Season with salt and pepper and serve.

POMMES DAUPHINE

Makes about 20 ovals

Basic Potato Gnocchi (page 97)

4 tablespoons butter

½ cup flour, plus more for rolling

Salt

3 egg yolks

Canola oil for frying

THESE DELECTABLE FRIED POTATO OVALS are a French bistro staple, and this is a venerable way to make them. Basically, our gnocchi dough is loosened with butter and eggs, rolled into small balls, and fried to make crispy fritters.

1. Prepare the Basic Potato Gnocchi dough through step 2.

2. Combine the butter and ½ cup water in a medium saucepan and bring to a boil. Reduce the heat to medium low and add the flour and ½ teaspoon salt, stirring with a wooden spoon. The mixture will pull away from the sides of the pan; continue to cook for 3–4 minutes. Add the egg yolks, one at a time, stirring constantly, until they are fully incorporated.

3. Fold the egg mixture into the gnocchi dough until thoroughly combined, adding more flour if the dough seems sticky. Dust your hands with flour and roll the dough into small balls or ovals.

4. To cook, heat about 4 inches of oil in a medium, heavy-bottomed saucepan until it reaches 325° on a candy thermometer. Drop the potato balls, a few at a time, into the hot oil. Fry until slightly puffed and golden brown, 4–6 minutes. With a slotted spoon, transfer to paper towels to drain. Repeat until all the balls are fried. Sprinkle with salt and serve.

BASIC POTATO GNOCCHI

Makes about 50 gnocchi, serving 6

1 pound medium Yukon Gold or yellow potatoes, peeled and quartered

4 egg yolks

½ cup flour, plus more for rolling

Pinch freshly ground nutmeg

Salt

BESIDES ITS CRUCIAL ROLE IN GNOCCHI, this basic potato dough is used in many of the recipes in this chapter, such as Schupfnudeln (page 100), Pommes Dauphine (page 94), and Potato-Leek Mezzalune (page 103). What's really important is to handle the dough while the potatoes are still warm. That way the egg yolks will "cook" in the warm potato mixture, tightening the dough and reducing the amount of extra flour needed; because the more flour you add, the more dense the dumpling will become. It's as simple as that. I like to serve these gnocchi with Mushroom Sauté (page 104), or just with a simple tomato sauce.

1. Put the potatoes in a large pot of cold water and bring to a boil. Reduce the heat and simmer until the potatoes are tender, about 15 minutes. Drain the potatoes and, while they are still hot, pass through a food mill or potato ricer into a large bowl.

2. Add the egg yolks, flour, and nutmeg and season with salt. Working quickly and gently, combine the ingredients with your hands until the mixture forms a ball and pulls away from the sides of the bowl. Add a bit more flour if the dough feels too sticky.

3. Turn the dough onto a well-floured surface, pat gently and divide. One at a time, roll each part into a long rope about ¾ inch thick. Cut the ropes into 1-inch pieces. Dust with more flour and roll each piece over a ribbed gnocchi board or over the tines of a fork to make their signature ridges.

4. To cook the gnocchi, bring a large pot of salted water to a gentle boil. Drop in the gnocchi and once they float to the surface, cook for another 30 seconds. Scoop them out with a slotted spoon. If using immediately, add them to a pan with sauce. If you're making them in advance, shock them in a bowl of ice water for a minute, then remove with a slotted spoon. Toss with a dash or two of oil, lay on a baking pan, and place in the freezer. When frozen, transfer to a resealable plastic bag and store in the freezer.

97

1. For the potato dough: Assemble the still-hot cooked potatoes, the egg yolks, flour, ground nutmeg, and salt, each in a separate bowl. Have a large mixing bowl ready for mixing the gnocchi dough.

4. Use flour sparingly, adding small handfuls at a time, mixing as you go, up to ½ cup. Add the nutmeg and salt.

5. Turn the potato dough onto a clean, lightly floured surface and gently pat to flatten.

2. Working quickly, spoon the hot potatoes into a food mill or a potato ricer and press to process.

3. Immediately add the 4 egg yolks to the warm, fluffy riced potatoes in the mixing bowl to "cook" the yolks.

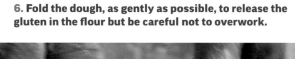

6. Fold the dough, as gently as possible, to release the gluten in the flour but be careful not to overwork.

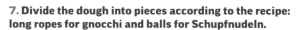

7. Divide the dough into pieces according to the recipe: long ropes for gnocchi and balls for Schupfnudeln.

SCHUPFNUDELN: LONG POTATO DUMPLINGS

Makes about 25

Basic Potato
Gnocchi (page 97)

¼ cup flour, plus
more for rolling

¼ teaspoon ground
turmeric

4 tablespoons butter

Salt

SCHUPFNUDELN—SLIM TAPERED NOODLES—are a specialty of the Baden region, home to the Spielweg. You use your palms to roll these dumplings and taper them on each end, like delicate little cigars. They most often accompany roasted or braised meats right on the plate because they do a great job of absorbing their juices, as in Blanquette de Veau (page 123).

1. Prepare the Basic Potato Gnocchi dough through step 2, adding an additional ¼ cup flour and using turmeric instead of the nutmeg. Mix until the dough pulls away from the sides of the bowl. Add a bit more flour if the dough seems too sticky to roll.

2. Divide the dough into 4 parts and on a lightly floured surface roll each into a long rope about ½ inch thick. Cut the ropes into 2-inch lengths. Dust your hands with flour and roll each piece between the palms of your hands to form tapered noodles, 3–4 inches long.

3. Boil as you would Basic Potato Gnocchi. Remove the noodles with a slotted spoon and drain on paper towels. Meanwhile, melt the butter in a large skillet over medium heat. Spoon the cooked noodles into the skillet and sauté until crispy and golden brown, about 3–5 minutes. Season with salt. Serve with your favorite sauce or meat.

POTATO-LEEK MEZZALUNE

Makes about 25, serving 4

¼ cup olive oil

2 leeks, washed and thinly sliced

Salt

Freshly ground black pepper

Basic Potato Gnocchi (page 97)

½ cup flour, plus more for rolling

4 tablespoons butter

THESE HALF-MOON RAVIOLIS are made from Basic Potato Gnocchi Dough (page 97) which is easily rolled out and cut into rounds for wrappers for other stuffed pasta or dumplings. They are equally interesting served as an appetizer or as a side dish with a main course. I vary the filling with the seasons, using about a half cup of sautéed greens, mushrooms, or squash—or even cheese.

1. Heat the olive oil in a medium skillet over medium heat. Add the leeks and cook, stirring occasionally, until tender, about 10 minutes. Season with salt and pepper and transfer to a bowl.

2. Prepare the Basic Potato Gnocchi dough through step 2, adding an additional ½ cup flour to the dough. Mix until the dough pulls away from the sides of the bowl. Add a bit more flour if the dough seems too sticky to roll.

3. Divide the dough into 2 portions. On a lightly floured surface, roll each portion into a large, thin sheet. Cut 4-inch rounds from the dough with a cookie cutter or drinking glass. Gather the trimmed dough

together and repeat until you've used all the dough.

4. To form the mezzalune, put a spoonful of the leeks into the center of one dough round. Fold into a half-moon and press the edges firmly with your fingers to seal. Repeat with the remaining dough rounds.

5. Bring a large pot of salted water to a boil. Drop in the mezzalune a few at a time. Once they have floated to the top, simmer for another 30 seconds. Meanwhile, melt the butter in a large skillet over medium-high heat. With a slotted spoon, drain and transfer the mezzalune to the skillet. Gently sauté each side until golden brown. Season with salt and pepper.

MUSHROOM SAUTÉ WITH GNOCCHI & PARMESAN

Serves 6

4 tablespoons butter

2 cloves garlic, sliced

Leaves from 4 sprigs fresh thyme

4 ounces wild mushrooms, such as porcinis and chanterelles, chopped

1 cup Basic Chicken Stock (page 250)

Salt

Freshly ground black pepper

Basic Potato Gnocchi (page 97)

Parmesan cheese, for shaving

AS SOON AS WILD MUSHROOMS begin appearing in the markets, it's this dish that leaps into my head.

1. Melt the butter in a large skillet over medium-high heat until brown and nutty. Add the garlic, thyme, and mushrooms and cook until the mushrooms are brown and soft, about 10 minutes. Add the Chicken Stock and cook until the broth is reduced by half. Season with salt and pepper.

2. Meanwhile, prepare the gnocchi according to the recipe. When done, scoop them right into the pan with the mushrooms. Toss until the gnocchi are well coated with sauce. Shave Parmesan over the gnocchi and serve.

ROAST FINGERLING POTATOES WITH LEMON & ROSEMARY

Serves 6

2 lemons

2 pounds fingerling potatoes, unpeeled

4 cloves garlic, peeled and crushed

3 tablespoons olive oil

2 sprigs fresh rosemary

Salt

Freshly ground black pepper

I LOVE TO ROAST THESE SMALL POTATOES right in the pan with the lovely Provençal Roast Leg of Lamb (page 172), the rustic Butcher Shop Chicken (page 172), or the big Côte de Boeuf (page 118), where they develop wonderfully crispy skins. But they can certainly be roasted and served on their own to delicious results.

1. Preheat the oven to 375°. Juice one lemon and quarter the other. In a bowl, toss the potatoes and garlic with the lemon juice, lemon quarters, olive oil, and rosemary. Season with salt and pepper.

2. Transfer the potatoes, lemons, and rosemary to a roasting pan (with or without meat) and roast, turning occasionally, until tender, about 25 minutes. Serve warm.

KARL-JOSEF'S POTATO SALAD

Serves 6

1½ pounds small yellow potatoes

2 tablespoons sunflower or canola oil

½ small onion, chopped

1 cup hot Basic Chicken Stock (page 250)

¼ cup apple cider vinegar

1 tablespoon Dijon mustard

Salt

Freshly ground black pepper

¼ cup fresh parsley leaves, thinly sliced

I HAD NEVER TASTED Karl-Josef's potato salad until we returned to the Spielweg to produce this book. When he learned I'd planned a chapter on potatoes, he insisted on making it for us. His surprise was to use hot stock to draw out the starch from the potatoes, lending creaminess to the salad. He adds the oil only after the seasonings have been absorbed by the potatoes, insisting that adding it earlier will inhibit that process.

1. Bring the potatoes to a boil in a large pot of cold salted water. Reduce the heat and simmer until tender, 15–20 minutes. Drain. When the potatoes are cool enough to handle, peel with a small knife and slice into a large bowl.

2. Heat 1 tablespoon of the oil in a small skillet over medium heat. Add the onions and cook until translucent, 3–4 minutes. Add the stock and bring to a boil.

3. To the potatoes in the bowl, add the hot stock and onions, the vinegar, mustard, and salt and pepper. Stir thoroughly, cover with plastic wrap, and let the potatoes sit for at least 30 minutes to absorb the seasonings. Stir in the remaining 1 tablespoon oil and the parsley and serve.

Curiosity

& the Cook

F

OR a skinny cook in
the Black Forest in 1993, this was heaven—or what
I assumed heaven could be, complete with free
Weizenbier (the typical southern German wheat
beer), wine that was cheaper than water, snow-
capped mountains in every direction, and cooking
and eating the kind of food that I'd only seen in
glossy periodicals. I had about eight weeks paid
vacation a year and I was actually in a place where
I had access to experiences greater than I'd ever
imagined: Italy was just four hours south, Paris four
hours to the west. What's more, I was exposed to
many meals I didn't cook at all; I merely enjoyed
them and they inspired me as much as if I had been
assisting the chef myself. Perhaps curiosity was one
of my greatest gifts. Dining with an ever-curious

**ON THE ROAD AGAIN, in a voluptuous Volnay vineyard, left, just outside
of Beaune, France. Overleaf, we would frequently escape across the border
to Alsace, to the vibrant Place de la Réunion in Mulhouse.**

"While I worked hard at the Spielweg all week long, I played hard every weekend, taking nothing for granted."

appetite, I was determined to take my great education to the next level. Almost every Saturday night, Jenifer and I would figure out where we'd dine the following week on my days off, scouring the atlas and the *Guide Michelin*. Certainly other deciding factors influenced where we'd go. For example, I was paid in Deutchmarks that had a favorable exchange rate in France and Italy, so we'd splurge after payday on the rare meal at a Michelin-starred icon. But more often we would immerse ourselves in the more bourgeois style of dining, which turned out to be just as rewarding: The quaint, low-ceilinged *winstubs* of Alsace all along the Route du Vin; the popular roadside bistros crowded with vineyard workers that decorate the slopes of the Côte de Beaune; the clubby *bouchons* of the Mâcon, whose proprietors knew every guest by name; and of course the polished Parisian brasserie giants like Au Pied de Cochon and Brasserie Lipp, specialists in everything pig and oyster long before the word gastropub was ever invented.

So while I worked hard at the Spielweg all week long, I played hard every weekend, taking nothing for granted. Even as we grew to love the beautiful mountain *Gasthauses* of the Black Forest and the warm trattorias of Northern Italy, it does say something about the French passion for food that dining at even the simplest of places was an experience of deep culinary discovery. Hence, Jenifer and I savored the French countryside and in fact we more or less lived across the Rhine in Alsace.

On our off nights, we'd head, not to the acclaimed Alsatian culinary capital of Strasbourg with its Michelin-starred restaurants, but to the charming smaller, and even closer, French town of Mulhouse, less than

AT EASE IN AVIGNON, 1996, far left. The Winstub Henriette, above and right, is still open in Mulhouse, serving specialties like munster cheese in pastry, below right.

an hour across the border. Just minutes away from our sleepy mountain hamlet of Spielweg with its gurgling streams and deep lush picturesque pastures, Jenifer and I would cross the Rhine near the ancient Roman-walled village of Breisach, where it seemed that every flower box was in perpetual bloom. Entering France we noticed that perhaps the villages were a little less "kept," graffiti more apparent, yes. But the people seemed happy and children would run freely through the streets. Even the adults seemed different here, with a uniquely French sense of style. It didn't seem possible that a mere river or national boundary could make such a difference in attitude, yet once you're in France you know it.

We crossed the river in our sputtering VW Jetta that had to be push-started (making parking it a particular challenge). Taking a deep liberating breath of French air, we steered toward Mulhouse, a town at the end of the Alsatian Route du Vin, and headed to an unassuming little bistro, the Winstub Henriette, which is still there today. The rue Henriette is just off the picture-perfect Place de la Réunion, the historic center of Mulhouse,

A FREQUENT STOP on the road to Mausanne and its beautiful olive oils is the extremely popular Bistrot du Paradou, above. On the terrace with Jen at La Cantonnade in Goudargues, left.

"Our little winstub was exactly what you picture when you think French bistro: dark yet homey, with an owner happy to take us into her perfect little world of hospitality."

now a brick-tiled pedestrian area of great charm with low townhouses meticulously repainted in the vivid colors of an opera set, facing the Hôtel de Ville, a vast pink pile built in 1430.

Without a doubt, our Louisiana heritage had much to do with our fondness for all things French. And as we later learned, Mulhouse, once an important center of textile manufacture, had ties, too, to Louisiana. Since it imported much of its cotton from our state, we thought of ourselves as long lost cousins! Certainly upon learning that we were from New Orleans, locals greeted us with such genuine warmth that it reaffirmed our desire to inhale all things French. Our little *winstub* was exactly what you picture when you think French bistro: narrow and dark yet homey, with an owner who was happy to greet us and to take us into her perfect little world of hospitality. Her style was uniquely hers: always high heels, always leopard-skin tights with an attitude to match; she was fearless, full of charm, and never without a smile. She struggled to understand us and would often resort to German in order to explain her menu of the day. I could understand her pleasant French, but the problem was that her menu was full of dishes I had never even heard of, much less experienced. Often without knowing what a dish was, we would order it anyway as a way to continue our voyage of discovery.

We'd order every part of the veal but the choice cuts, *rognons de veau, blanquette de veau,* brains, and sweetbreads. And slowly, over the course of a year, I developed a passion for these very delicious *spécialités d'Alsace:* platters of poached river pike over buttery potatoes bathed in brown butter, capers, and meticulously minced parsley with the obligatory squeeze of lemon; casseroles of *Baeckeoffe,* a soulful stew of pork, beef, and lamb shoulder slowly cooked with white wine, potatoes, leeks, and carrots and perfumed with juniper berries. *Foie de veau,* or calf's liver, sautéed in butter and finished with onions, beef marrow, and pinot noir; *Maultaschen,* pinwheel raviolis served whole in broth or sliced with a sauce. Snails from the nearby vineyards and plump frogs' legs—both cooked any way imaginable, from a *civet* (stew) of white wine to a sauté with butter, garlic, and thyme. Rabbits, as in my native Louisiana, were normally slow-cooked in either red or white wine until the tender flesh just eased from the bone, then served over pillowy potato dumplings that absorbed the delicate flavors of the herby gravy. Desserts were of a similar honesty, but focused on the purity of delicious eggs, cream, and sugar. A perfect example was the subtly flavored pots de crème (page 269) that, in spite of their simplicity, become heavenly and sinful with every delicious spoonful. My meals at the Winstub Henriette may have not been served with the pomp of the great Alsatian dining rooms, but they offered this poor cook true insight into the soul of a French cuisine that has forever flavored my food. In fact it was the cooking of Alsace (as well as the brasserie traditions of early New Orleans) that directly influenced our restaurant Lüke. Have I told you how important it is to keep yourself open to discovery, no matter where it takes you?

BAECKEOFFE: A MEATY STEW

Serves 8

2 medium onions, chopped

2 medium leeks, chopped

1 stalk celery, chopped

4 carrots, chopped

4 cloves garlic, finely chopped

1 bay leaf

2 sprigs fresh thyme

1 sprig fresh marjoram

3 juniper berries, crushed

Pinch red pepper flakes

1 bottle white wine

1 pound beef chuck, cut into small pieces

1 pound pork shoulder, cut into small pieces

1 pound lamb shoulder, cut into small pieces

1 pig's foot

Salt

Freshly ground black pepper

2 tablespoons olive oil

2 pounds fingerling potatoes

1 cup Basic Fond de Veau (page 121) or Basic Veal Stock (page 250)

THIS SUCCULENT STEW IS ONE of the quintessential dishes of Alsace in which the cheaper cuts of pork and lamb are transformed. *Baeckeoffe* dates from the time farmers' wives would bring their earthenware pots to the village baker's oven to cook. The baker would seal each pot with a rim of pastry to keep in the flavors during the long cooking. I fell in love with *Baeckeoffe* at the Winstub Henriette before I even knew what a classic it was. I still love to cook it up on a cold day.

1. Combine the onions, leeks, celery, carrots, garlic, bay leaf, thyme, marjoram, juniper berries, red pepper, and 3 cups of the wine in a large bowl. Add the beef, pork, lamb, and pig's foot and season generously with salt and pepper. Cover and marinate overnight in the refrigerator.

2. Preheat the oven to 350°. Put the oil in a large, heavy-bottomed pot. Then, layer in the meat and vegetables and the potatoes. Pour the marinade into the pot and add the remaining wine and the Fond de Veau. Cover and bring to a simmer on the stove. Transfer to the oven and braise 3–3½ hours.

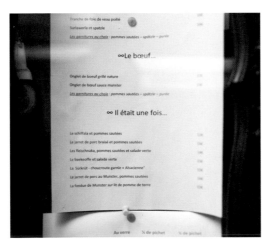

PIEDS DE COCHON GRILLÉ WITH BÉARNAISE SAUCE

Serves 6

Olive oil

2 onions, chopped

1 carrot, chopped

1 stalk celery, chopped

1 bay leaf

2 sprigs fresh thyme

6 cups Basic Chicken Stock (page 250)

6 pigs' feet, split in half

Salt

Freshly ground black pepper

FOR THE BÉRNAISE SAUCE

¼ cup white wine

¼ cup white wine vinegar

1 shallot, finely chopped

A few whole black peppercorns

2 egg yolks

½ cup (1 stick) butter

Salt

Leaves from 5 sprigs fresh tarragon, chopped

Squeeze of lemon juice

Tabasco

OF ALL OF THE GREAT, GUTSY BRASSERIE DISHES, pigs' feet is one of my favorites. I return to the Parisian brasseries that serve them as often as I can. This is where a good butcher comes in handy; he will have access to beautiful pigs' feet that just aren't available in the supermarket. Ask him to split the pigs' feet in half, making both cooking and eating them so much easier.

1. For the pigs' feet, heat the oil in a large, heavy-bottomed pot over medium-high heat. Add the onions, carrots, and celery and cook until tender, about 10 minutes. Add the bay leaf, thyme, Chicken Stock, and pigs' feet and bring to a boil. Reduce the heat, cover, and simmer about 2 hours. Remove the feet from the pot, season with salt and pepper, and set aside.

2. For the Béarnaise Sauce, combine the wine, vinegar, shallot, and peppercorns in a small saucepan over medium heat. Bring to a boil and reduce for 5–7 minutes. Strain the liquid into a bowl and add the egg yolks and 1 tablespoon water. Set the bowl over a pot of simmering water and whisk vigorously for 5 minutes. Warm the butter in another small saucepan so that it's hot to the touch, about 140°. Whisk the hot butter into the egg yolks in a slow, steady stream, until all the butter is incorporated and the sauce is thickened. Season with salt and add the tarragon, a small squeeze of lemon, and a dash of Tabasco.

3. Prepare a charcoal or gas grill or heat a grill pan on high. Put the feet on the grill and char on all sides, about 5 minutes. Serve with the Béarnaise Sauce.

BAGUETTES ON A BIKE in Beaune. Doesn't get more French than that.

117

CÔTE DE BOEUF
WITH RED WINE & PORCINI MUSHROOMS

Serves 8–10

1 4–5-pound bone-in rib roast

Salt

Freshly ground black pepper

½ cup red wine

4 tablespoons butter

8 porcini mushrooms, thickly sliced

1 shallot, minced

Leaves from 4 sprigs fresh thyme

1 cup Basic Fond de Veau (page 121)

I WASN'T CRAZY ABOUT BEEF until I discovered the flavor of Charolais beef in France. *Côte de boeuf* literally means "cut of beef," which here indicates a small standing rib roast. I combine the drippings from the roast with red wine and Fond de Veau to make a rich mushroom sauce, wonderful with the roast beef. If porcinis are not in season, use whatever combination of wild and domestic mushrooms you can find (even rehydrated dried porcinis in the mix will enrich the flavor)—just make sure there are plenty of them.

1. Preheat the oven to 400°. Season the rib roast generously with salt and pepper and place in a roasting pan. Roast until the beef is browned on the outside and medium rare on the inside with an internal temperature of 130°, about 45 minutes.

2. Transfer the roast to a platter. Deglaze the roasting pan with the wine, scraping up any delicious browned bits from the bottom of the pan. Then, melt the butter in a skillet over medium-high heat. Add the mushrooms and brown on both sides, about 5 minutes. Add the shallots and thyme, then the wine from the pan and the Fond de Veau. Simmer until the mushrooms are tender, about 5 minutes. Season with salt and pepper. Serve with the roast.

CHOUCROUTE GARNIE

Serves 8–10

2 tablespoons vegetable oil

4 onions, chopped

1 carrot, chopped

1 stalk celery, chopped

Salt

Freshly ground black pepper

2 cups dry Riesling

1 pound pork belly

8 ounces slab bacon, diced

1 ham hock

6 cups sauekraut, rinsed and squeezed dry

1 teaspoon caraway seeds

2 juniper berries, crushed

1 bay leaf

4 medium yellow potatoes, peeled and quartered

1 pound bratwurst links (about 4)

1 pound garlic sausage

2 tablespoons honey

CHOUCROUTE, LIKE MANY PEASANT FOODS, is best served family style—on a huge platter of sauerkraut studded with sausages and bacon. Here, a more demure portion at Winstub Henriette in Mulhouse. Search your farmers markets for artisanal fermented sauerkraut, you'll find its deep flavor makes all the difference.

1. Preheat the oven to 350°. Heat the oil in a medium heavy-bottomed pot over medium heat. Add half the onions, the carrots, and celery and cook until tender, about 10 minutes. Season with salt and pepper. Add 2 cups water, the wine, and pork belly and bring to a boil. Cover, transfer to the oven, and braise until the belly is tender, about 2 hours. Let cool in the braising liquid. Set the pork belly aside, then strain and reserve the liquid.

2. Render the bacon in a heavy-bottomed pot over medium-high heat. Add the remaining onions and cook until tender, about 10 minutes. Reduce the heat to medium, add the braised pork belly, ham hock, sauerkraut, caraway seeds, juniper berries, and bay leaf. Cover with the reserved braising liquid and bring to a boil. Reduce the heat and simmer about 45 minutes.

3. Add the potatoes, bratwurst, garlic sausage, and honey to the sauerkraut, cover, and steam together for 30 minutes more.

4. To serve, slice the pork belly into serving pieces. Discard the bay leaf. Mound the sauerkraut on a generous platter and pile the meat and potatoes on top.

1. For a deep flavor, caramelize the onions, carrots, celery, and garlic, stirring constantly, until dark brown.

2. After toasting the tomato paste with the caramelized vegetables, deglaze the pot with the wine.

3. Add the deeply roasted veal shanks to the vegetables and reduced wine in the pot.

4. Cover with the Veal Stock, bring to a boil, and add the bay leaf, thyme, and black peppercorns.

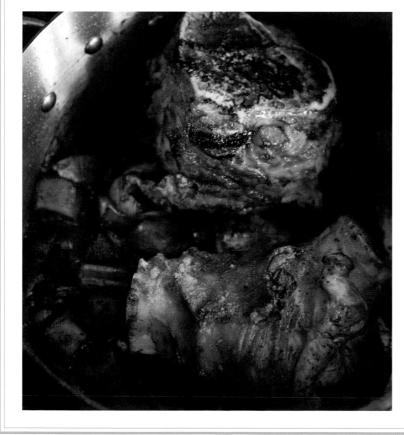

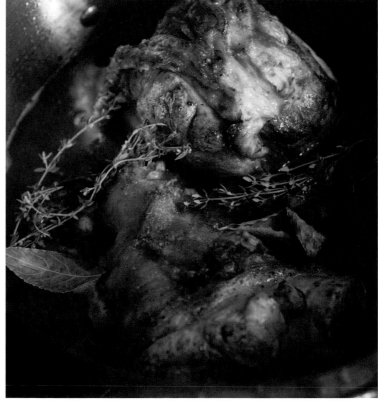

BASIC FOND DE VEAU

Makes about 4 cups

3 pounds veal bones or shanks

3 tablespoons olive oil

2 large onions, roughly chopped

1 carrot, roughly chopped

1 stalk celery, roughly chopped

1 head garlic, halved

2 tablespoons tomato paste

2 cups red wine

8 cups Basic Veal Stock (page 250)

1 bay leaf

4 sprigs fresh thyme

1 teaspoon black peppercorns

THIS SAUCE IS THE COOK'S BEST FRIEND and the building block of many great French dishes. The powdered stuff sold in stores is not even in the same ballpark. This *fond*, or foundation sauce, takes my Basic Veal Stock (page 250) then flavors and reduces it to intensify its power. Fond de Veau does require a bit of preparation and is probably the most expensive sauce I use, but it is so worth it for the potent, authentic flavor it confers to something as simple as sautéed porcini mushrooms (page 118) or as literally the secret sauce in the Ragout of Lamb (page 171).

1. Preheat the oven to 425°. Place the bones on a baking pan and roast until dark brown, about 45 minutes. Meanwhile, heat the oil in a large, heavy-bottomed pot over medium-high heat. Add onions and cook, stirring, until caramelized, 15–20 minutes. Add the carrots, celery, and garlic and cook until browned, about 15 minutes more.

2. Add the tomato paste and toast until it turns a dark, mahogany color. Add the wine and bring to a boil, scraping up the browned bits from the bottom of the pot. Add the roasted bones, Veal Stock, bay leaf, thyme, and peppercorns. Bring to a boil, reduce the heat, and simmer until the Fond de Veau is rich, dark brown, and reduced by half, about 4 hours. Strain and cool. Store in the freezer in small batches.

BLANQUETTE DE VEAU

Serves 6

4 tablespoons butter

1 onion, chopped

1 large leek, chopped

1 stalk celery, chopped

4 cloves garlic, chopped

1 sprig fresh thyme

1 bay leaf

4 cups Basic Veal Stock (page 250)

2 pounds veal breast, cut into 2-inch pieces

12 small carrots, peeled and left whole

6 small turnips, peeled and halved

½ cup pearl onions, peeled

4 porcini mushrooms, halved

3 egg yolks

½ cup heavy cream

Salt

Freshly ground black pepper

A GOOD VEAL STOCK is the secret of this unctuous veal stew. The word *blanquette* tells us this is a refined, white veal stew. Cooked properly, the veal and its stock have a gorgeous silky texture which is enhanced by the delicate flavors of the mushrooms and the small root vegetables.

1. Heat the butter in a large, heavy-bottomed pot over medium heat. Add the onions, leeks, celery, and garlic, plus a bit of oil if needed, and cook until tender, about 10 minutes. Add the thyme, bay leaf, Veal Stock, and veal and bring gently to a boil. Reduce the heat, cover, and simmer until the veal is tender, 50–60 minutes, skimming the fat as it rises to the surface.

2. Add the carrots, turnips, pearl onions, and mushrooms and simmer until tender, another 15 minutes.

3. Mix the egg yolks with the cream in a small bowl. Add a cup of hot stock and whisk well. Then slowly whisk the cream mixture back into the simmering pot. Season with salt and pepper, discard the bay leaf and thyme sprig, and serve.

WHAT'S MY FAVORITE wood fired pizza place in the South of France, you might ask? Easy: Chez Jo in Aix-en-Provence, source of this pilfered placemat.

POT AU FEU OF TONGUE

Serves 6–8

2 tablespoons
olive oil

2 medium onions,
chopped

1 stalk celery,
chopped

1 carrot, peeled and
chopped

12 cups Basic Chicken
Stock (page 250)

1 sprig fresh thyme

1 bay leaf

Salt

Freshly ground
black pepper

1 3-pound calf
tongue

2 medium yellow
potatoes, diced
small

1 celery root, peeled
and diced small

1 leek, chopped

1 knob fresh
horseradish, peeled
and grated

ONE OF THE GREAT DISCOVERIES I MADE when I first started exploring small French bistros was how delicious the off-cuts like tongue can be, and how little-appreciated they are in America. This presentation of tongue sliced in its own light broth is surprisingly delicate.

1. Heat the oil in a large, heavy-bottomed pot over medium heat. Add the onions, celery, and carrots and cook until the onions are translucent and the vegetables are tender, 5–7 minutes. Add the Chicken Stock, thyme, and bay leaf and season with salt and pepper. Add the tongue, bring the stock to a boil, then reduce to a simmer. Cover and cook for 2½ hours.

2. Transfer the tongue to a large bowl. Strain the stock and return to the pot. Add the potatoes, celery root, and leeks and simmer in the liquid as the tongue cools. When the tongue is cool enough to handle, peel and discard the skin. When the vegetables are tender, slice the tongue thinly at an angle. Spoon vegetables, broth, and the tongue into bowls and top with freshly grated horseradish.

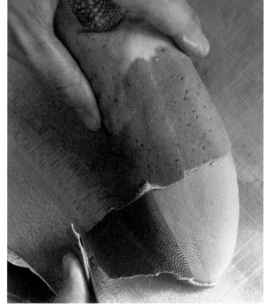

MAULTASCHEN: STUFFED PASTA

Serves 6

FOR THE PASTA
DOUGH

2 cups flour, plus
more for rolling

Salt

2 eggs

1 tablespoon
canola oil

FOR THE FILLING

1 piece country
bread, torn into
small pieces

⅓ cup milk

2 pounds spinach,
stems removed

4 slices bacon,
chopped

1 onion, chopped

1 clove garlic,
chopped

1 egg

1 pound ground beef

Leaves from
2 sprigs fresh
thyme, chopped

Generous pinch
ground nutmeg

Generous pinch
ground mace

Salt

Freshly ground
black pepper

6 cups Basic Veal
Stock (page 250)

THIS STUFFED PASTA has been a favorite ever since I first encountered it at Winstub Henriette. Karl-Josef makes it at the Spielweg, but only for family meal. It is a kind of a peasant-style pasta that is eaten either in the stock it's poached in, or after poaching, sliced and sautéed and served with tomato and fresh herbs. When I go through the process of making this pasta, I like to double the recipe and store a batch in the freezer. We serve it at our restaurant Lüke in New Orleans and occasionally at August.

1. For the dough, combine the flour, salt, eggs, and oil in a large bowl. Mix with your hands to make a soft dough. On a well-floured surface, knead until smooth and shiny, about 10 minutes. Divide the dough into two balls and wrap in plastic while you make the filling.

2. For the filling, combine the bread and milk in a bowl and allow the bread to soak up all the milk; set aside. Bring a large pot of salted water to a boil, add the spinach, and cook about 1 minute. Drain and squeeze out the water; chop and set aside. Cook the bacon in a large skillet over medium heat until crisp. Add the onions and garlic and cook until soft, about 5 minutes. Transfer the onions to the bowl of a food processor and add the soaked bread, spinach, egg, ground beef, thyme, nutmeg,

and mace. Blend until the mixture is thoroughly combined and season with salt and pepper.

3. Roll half the dough into a 12- by 18-inch rectangle about ⅛ inch thick. Spread half the filling over the dough, leaving an inch border around the edges. Brush the edges with water and roll the filled dough into a log, starting on a short edge. Repeat with the remaining dough and filling. The rolls are too big to poach in one piece, so I cut them into 3-inch sections.

4. Bring the Veal Stock to a simmer in a large saucepan and season with salt and pepper. In batches, add the stuffed pasta rolls and simmer for about 12 minutes. Drain. Slice and serve in a bowl with some of the cooking liquid or, as I like it, with a simple tomato and basil sauce.

ROASTED MARROW BONES WITH BRIOCHE

Serves 6

6 pounds marrow
  bones, split in half
  lengthwise

Coarse sea salt

Freshly ground
  black pepper

3 brioche rolls,
  sliced and grilled

THIS IS A TREAT THAT MY GOOD FRIEND Bertrand Béraud would serve to those
lucky guests who happened to visit his house in the Loire. It is so easy to prepare,
just spooning soft marrow from broiled bones onto crispy brioche, and so luscious.

1. Put the oven rack on the top shelf and
preheat the broiler. Place the bones, marrow side up, on a baking pan and season
with salt and pepper. Broil the bones until
the marrow is molten and bubbly, about 10
minutes.

2. Serve the marrow bones with the grilled
brioche and more coarse sea salt.

PROVENÇAL CAILLETTES WITH WHOLE GRAIN MUSTARD

Serves 8–10

1½ pounds ground
pork

8 ounces chicken
livers

4 ounces ground
pork fat

2 eggs

¼ cup white wine

¼ cup dry bread
crumbs

2 cups wilted
spinach, chopped

1 shallot, finely
chopped

2 green onions,
chopped

2 cloves garlic, finely
chopped

Leaves from 4
sprigs fresh thyme

1 sprig fresh
tarragon, chopped

Salt

Freshly ground
black pepper

6 pieces pork caul
fat, rinsed and
soaked in water

2 tablespoons herbes
de Provence

Whole grain
mustard and
crusty bread

CAILLETTES ARE FREE-FORM PEASANT-STYLE PÂTÉS, on sale at most every Provençal butcher shop and charcuterie. Usually based on pork, the butcher often adds off-cuts like sweetbreads. They're full of green herbs and almost always eaten chilled or at room temperature. Sliced, with mustard and lots of crusty bread, they are a great first course. Chef Chris would make *caillettes* and give them away to his friends, a tradition I sorely miss.

1. Preheat the oven to 350°. Combine all the ingredients up to the caul fat in the bowl of a food processor and blend until thoroughly combined. Divide the mixture into 6 balls, wrap each in a piece of caul fat, and place on a baking pan, seam side down.

2. Dust the tops of each *caillette* with the herbes de Provence. Bake until browned, about 45 minutes. Remove from the oven and cool. Serve with mustard and crusty bread.

ON THE BANKS of the lovely Cèze in Goudargues are restaurants I'd escape to while working at the nearby Chateau de Montcaud.

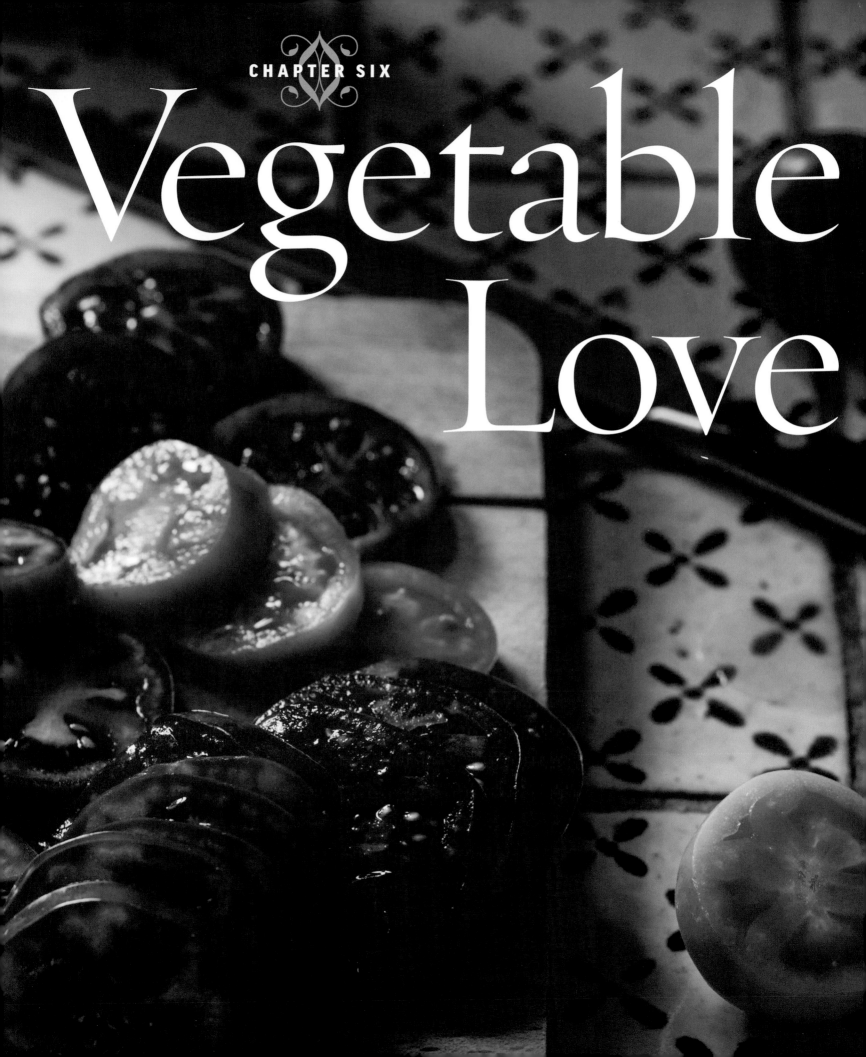

CHAPTER SIX

Vegetable Love

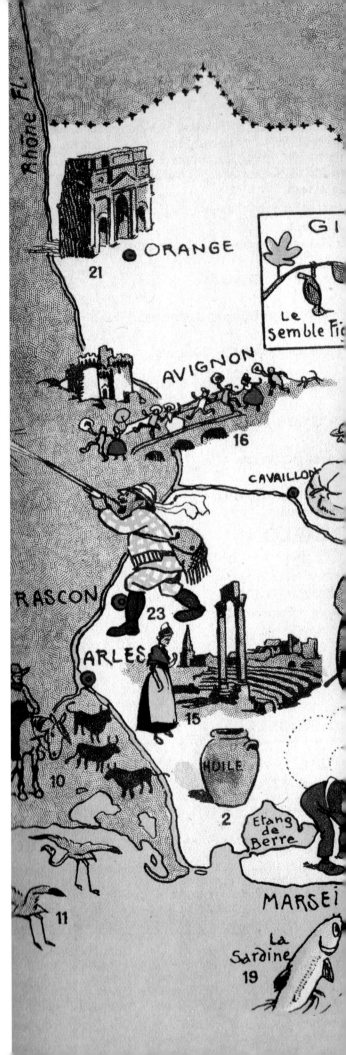

I HAD ONLY A slim balance at the Untermünstertal branch of the prestigious Volksbank when I embarked on my first journey to Provence. But as close to broke as I was in a financial sense, my romanticism for the fancy sleeper car from Basel to Marseille overrode any sort of logic. Certainly, this was not the top-of-the-line Orient Express I had dreamed of, but rather a local SNCF train that would provide the redemptive passage from the chilly, wet, and grey foothills of the Alps to the ever-sunny and always-wonderful South of France. Just married and never having enjoyed a lavish excursion before, I thought, Okay, the time to splurge is now! So I went for it: the sleeper car for me and my baby, where we'd lounge and love with Champagne (or a cheaper substitute), all the way to Provence in a style to make James Bond envious.

MY PROVENCE on one map, right. Overleaf, my Provence on one counter.

"*Although I'd set the bar high, Provence did not disappoint. We were in awe from the moment we descended the train at the sun-drenched Marseille station.*"

Gliding up the steps, negotiating the half-broken door in the process, tickets in one hand and young gorgeous bride in the other, I tried to overlook the soot and scuffed-up, low-quality finishes of our "sleeper car." But it was impossible not to notice what smelled like a wrestling team chain-smoking rank Turkish cigarettes—thanks to the six fellows who just happened to be our sleeper car mates. Okay, I'm thinking, this is no place for my sweet little Southern wife, who had to be practically dragged from Daddy, kicking and screaming, all the way to Germany. Our first trip to Provence and we already had the makings of a *Seinfeld* episode. This was not going to work. We politely excused ourselves and found the bar car, which turned out not to be a lounge car as the sign indicated, but a bar in the shadiest sense. It did, however, offer refuge, warmth, and liquor that quickly worked its magic, helping us dream away the next twelve hours as we traversed the lush mountain pastures to the stark, steely-white, rocky outcroppings of the South. We sat on our cramped vinyl banquette, talking and planning every step of our vacation with travel books, novels, and maps spread out on the worn veneer of our bar table.

Over the past year, 1993, while living, working, and learning in our little mountain hamlet of Spielweg, we had devoured food and travel books, including M.F.K. Fisher's wonderful *Long Ago in France,* about her years in Dijon, as well as *Serve It Forth* and *The Gastronomical Me;* Patricia Wells's *Food Lover's Guide to France;* and Peter Mayle's *A Year in Provence,* plus the Michelin green and red guides, and Gayot's guide to France's top tables. Certainly my reading had not a little to do with my romanticizing most things French and all things Provençal. Already familiar with Alsace, Burgundy, and even Paris, we were both so excited about exploring this mythical land that seemed to combine the most perfect parts of France, Italy, and Spain. Based on our reading, we decided to carefully choreograph our trip to experience the famed farmers' markets of such iconic Provençal villages as St.-Rémy-de-Provence, Arles, Cavaillon, Aix-en-Provence, Apt, Gordes, and Avignon, among others. We made itineraries noting each village, its market days, which grand restaurants were nearby, and most important, were they open for lunch? (Our budget never allowed us to have dinner in a prestigious place, but lunch we could swing.) For dinner, we'd retire to our rented *gîte rural,* a country refuge, where we'd roll up our sleeves, cook rustic Provençal dinners from what the market provided, drink *vin de pays,* and dine under the stars.

My expectations were inflated because of those incredible culinary literary works that I absorbed so effortlessly. But although I'd set the bar high, Provence did not disappoint. We were in absolute awe from the moment we descended the train at the sun-drenched Marseille station, where the briny air immediately spoke to my New Orleans sensibilities. Loud voices whipped through like a Mediterranean breeze filled with passionate shouts and jeers in French, Provençal, Greek, Spanish, Arabic, and Italian. The predictable smells of tobacco, coffee,

A CATHEDRAL of sycamores, plane trees, near St. Rémy.

FIRST TRIP TO PROVENCE, 1994, Jen and I get haircuts, above. The best olive oil makers in France, left, are in the Valley of Les Baux, in Maussane. The Saturday market in Apt, right, is crazy, sprawling, exciting, and not-to-be missed.

and freshly baked bread mixing with diesel fumes made me feel right at home, even though nothing I had read prepared me for this. Provence was already different from any France I had ever known.

We eventually made our way to our rustic *mas,* a small farmhouse in the jagged granite hills south of the fashionable village of St.-Rémy-de-Provence. On either side of the old farmhouse stood orchards of apples and apricots and olive groves that really are as silver as Van Gogh saw them. Our stone dwelling, with rustic timbers and walls a yard thick, was built from the same stone that the Phoenicians and Romans had used to build on these same hills. Much has been written about St.-Rémy. In fact, its Wednesday market has by now become something of a cliché and, I would argue, for good cause. The fact is that beautiful, well-heeled people do abound, and

chic Parisians and New Yorkers do tend to flit about as if on social calls, occupying the most coveted tables around the boulevards Mirabeau and Gambetta. Yet despite all this glamour, pomp, and circumstance, which bothered me not at all, I came to know Vegetable Love.

France is full of all the things you really don't need. If it's a luxury, France is the best place to find it: fine art, jewelry, ballet, wine, cognac, Champagne; and designer everything from underwear to shoes, from perfume to pâté de foie gras. At the market in St.-Rémy, accompanied by Jenifer, her basket, and a ravenous hunger, for the first time I considered vegetables to be a luxury, too. Browsing this quintessential Provençal market, with sprawling stalls that seem to occupy every square inch of the town and the most perfect vegetables and fruits seductively arranged, it quickly became obvious that

French farmers are geniuses at display. And that's when I found myself, surprisingly, flirting with a vegetable. It was the aubergines that first caught my eye. Never had I seen so many varieties of eggplants, so perfectly picked and groomed, displayed in small baskets tenderly lined to protect their sensitive skins. The slender, midnight blue specimens were the first to intrigue me, but I didn't yet know what to do with those Asian varieties. I had my heart set on the small, oblong, and striped eggplants perfect for the *petit farci* I was craving. I asked the farmer politely for a half dozen, knowing that I'd prepare them stuffed with a mixture of bread crumbs, grated cheese, garlic, and fresh wild herbs, perfumed with olive oil from Maussane.

I picked up a large eggplant, deep purple, round and smooth, and found it heavy in my hand, just about half the size of a football. I knew I'd roast and purée it with garlic and more olive oil to make my creamy *caviar d'aubergine*—a perfect hors d'oeuvre to enjoy while cooking or playing *pétanque*. But what about those young, slender, and oh-so-curvy eggplants snuggling under the cool shade of a mammoth umbrella protecting them from harmful UV rays? I could not just walk away. There had to be something I could do with them. In a flash I knew what they were destined to be: ratatouille! So tender and delicate, they would be so succulent cooked down with sweet onions, tiny red and yellow bell peppers, young garlic, zucchini, and basil with those voluptuous, end-of-summer tomatoes that bordered on over-ripeness, just picked from the vine a moment before being carried off to the market. So love won, and for that evening we became vegetarians. And happy, lucky ones at that. Provence, *je t'aime!*

GRILLED ARTICHOKES WITH LEMON

Serves 4

4 medium artichokes

3 lemons

Olive oil

Salt

Freshly ground black pepper

Leaves from 1 sprig fresh rosemary, chopped

Leaves from 2 sprigs fresh thyme, chopped

4 green onions, chopped

FOR ME, THE BEST WAY TO CELEBRATE the beauty of artichokes (preferably the elegant, long-stemmed, purple-tinged variety you find in Provence) is to slice them lengthwise to reveal their beautiful interiors. Then, brush with oil and lay on a grill to gently char.

1. If you're lucky enough to find young artichokes with long stems, peel the skins from the stems. Bring a large pot of salted water to a boil and squeeze in the juice of 1 lemon. Add the artichokes and simmer until they are almost tender, about 7 minutes; drain. Slice in half lengthwise and scoop out the choke with a spoon if using large artichokes.

2. Prepare a charcoal or gas grill, or heat a grill pan over high heat. Drizzle both sides of the artichokes with olive oil, season with salt and pepper, and put them directly on the grill, cut sides down. Grill until they are slightly charred and tender, about 5 minutes. Remove the artichokes from the grill, shine them with olive oil, give them a squeeze of lemon juice, and scatter the rosemary, thyme, and green onions on top. Serve with lemon wedges.

FAVA BEANS ON THE GRILL

Serves 6

2 pounds fresh fava
beans, unpeeled,
rinsed and dried

Olive oil

Salt

Freshly ground
black pepper

Juice of 1 lemon

I LOVE TO MAKE THESE FAVAS in the heart of their season when I'm about to fire up the grill for dinner. They are a lot of fun to peel with your fingers, a casual hors d'oeuvre with a glass of wine.

1. Prepare a charcoal or gas grill or heat a grill pan over high heat. In a bowl, toss the fava beans with a generous amount of olive oil and season with salt and pepper. Put them directly on the grill and cook, turning every several minutes, until they are well charred and blistered, 5–8 minutes. Remove from the grill, toss with the lemon juice, and serve.

FAVA BEAN & TOMATO RAGOUT

Serves 6

4 pounds fresh fava
beans, shucked

3 tablespoons
olive oil

2 cloves garlic,
thinly sliced

1 anchovy filet,
minced

6 plum tomatoes,
peeled and
chopped

Pinch red pepper
flakes

Salt

Freshly ground
black pepper

Zest of 1 lemon

Leaves from
4 sprigs fresh mint,
chopped

FINDING FRESH FAVA BEANS is not always easy, especially when they're out of season. When I can't find them, I use fresh or frozen edamame.

1. Drop the fava beans into a large pot of boiling salted water and simmer for 30 seconds. Remove, let them cool for a minute, then use your fingers to pull away the outer shell and pop out the bright green beans.

2. Heat the oil in a large, heavy-bottomed saucepan over medium-high heat. Add the garlic and anchovy and cook, stirring constantly, until the anchovy has melted into the oil, about 2 minutes. Add the tomatoes and red pepper flakes and cook, stirring constantly, for another 2–3 minutes. Add the favas and season with salt and pepper. Reduce the heat to medium and cook for another 5 minutes. Stir in the lemon zest and mint and serve.

TOMATO & FRESH CHEESE TARTINES

Serves 6

1 loaf crusty bread, sliced

Olive oil

4 cloves garlic, peeled

8 ounces fresh ricotta

4 ripe tomatoes, different colors and sizes, sliced

Salt

Freshly ground black pepper

¼ cup Black Olive Tapenade (page 215)

Small fresh mint, basil leaves, and chopped fresh chives, for garnish

IN FRANCE I love to use Brousse, the simple fresh cheese made from the whey of goat's milk, from goats that graze on the rocky, herb-covered hills above Marseille. But at home I always use the best, fresh-made ricotta I can find and no one knows the difference.

1. Preheat the oven to 325°. Drizzle the bread slices with olive oil. Place on a baking dish and toast in the oven on both sides. Rub the toasts with the garlic cloves, then spread on the cheese.

2. Layer the tomato slices on top of the toasts and sprinkle with a little salt and pepper. Drizzle with a generous amount of olive oil, top with spoonfuls of tapenade, and sprinkle basil leaves and chives on top.

OUR LOCAL produce market, just outside the melon-rich town of Cavaillon.

142

EGGPLANT, SUMMER SQUASH & TOMATO TIAN

Serves 6–8

1 large eggplant

1 medium zucchini

1 medium yellow summer squash

4 medium tomatoes

3 tablespoons olive oil, plus more for the tian

1 medium onion, thinly sliced

2 cloves garlic, thinly sliced

4 eggs

1 cup cream

¼ cup grated Parmesan cheese

Leaves from 2 sprigs fresh basil, chopped

2 pinches crushed red pepper flakes

Salt

Freshly ground black pepper

THE KEY TO THIS DISH is to precook the eggplant to remove any bitterness before assembling the tian. The proportions of the vegetables don't matter much, though I love to mix the summer colors of zucchini, tomato, and golden summer squash. You can use all zucchini or none at all. I make this tian when garden vegetables are at their peak ripeness.

1. Preheat the oven to 350°. Slice the eggplant, zucchini, summer squash, and tomatoes crosswise into ½-inch-thick slices. Heat the oil in a large skillet over medium-high heat. In batches, add the eggplant slices and cook, flipping once, until both sides are golden brown, about 5 minutes. Drain on paper towels and sprinkle with salt.

2. Oil a large baking dish or tian. Make a pinwheel pattern of the eggplant, zucchini, summer squash, and tomato slices, layering in the onions and garlic, until all the vegetables are used.

3. Whisk together the eggs, cream, Parmesan, basil, and red pepper, season with salt and pepper, and pour into the baking dish. Bake the tian until the vegetables are tender, the custard is set, and the top is nicely browned, 45 minutes to 1 hour. Serve right from the baking dish.

145

SPRING SPINACH, NETTLES, & DANDELION GREENS TIAN

Serves 6-8

3 tablespoons olive oil, plus more for the baking dish

1 clove garlic

2 bunches spring greens, such as dandelions and nettles, washed and chopped

1 bunch spring spinach, washed and chopped

3 eggs

¾ cup cream

Salt

Freshly ground black pepper

I MAKE THIS GREEN TIAN when the first early spring and summer tender greens come to market. I like to use a mixture of bitter and mellow greens: the earliest spinach, tiny dandelion greens, and stinging nettles. Or use sorrel, kale, mustard, and/or turnip greens. Whatever looks bright and irresistible.

1. Preheat the oven to 350°. To clean the nettles, use gloves to pull the leaves from the stems, then put them in a bowl of cold water and swish with tongs.

2. Heat the oil in a large skillet over medium-high heat. Add the garlic, then the greens and spinach and cook until wilted, 3–4 minutes.

3. In a large bowl, whisk together the eggs and cream and season with salt and pepper. Add the wilted greens and all of their juices and mix well. Brush the inside of a large baking dish or tian with olive oil and pour the mixture into dish. Bake for 30 minutes or until the tian has set.

ON TIANS

IN THIS COUNTRY, baking dishes like these, above, seem to only appear at holiday dinners. But in Provence, a tian, a baked vegetable dish named for the vessel it's cooked in, is served every day in so many ways.

The common thread that runs through all the tians in this book is a light custard of eggs and milk or cream that binds the vegetables together.

BRAISED FENNEL

Serves 6-8

3-4 medium fennel
bulbs

Salt

¼ cup olive oil

¼ cup Basic Chicken
Stock (page 250)
or water

Juice of 1 lemon

1 tablespoon
vermouth

2 cloves garlic, sliced

2 sprigs fresh thyme

BRAISED FENNEL IS A FINE ACCOMPANIMENT to lamb. At home I make a variation of this dish where I'll add ½ cup of cream and ¼ cup grated Parmesan before the dish goes into the oven. The melted Parmesan forms a delicious crust. I like to use fennel stalks or fronds in any number of recipes, from Soupe de Poisson (page 237) to stuffing whole grilled fish (page 60). The easiest way to keep fennel stalks is in a resealable plastic bag in the freezer.

1. Preheat the oven to 325°. Trim the fennel fronds and reserve for another use. Halve the bulbs and cut into quarters. Bring a medium pot of salted water to a boil. Drop in the fennel and simmer until the bulbs can be easily pierced with the tip of a small knife, 5–8 minutes. Drain.

2. Put the fennel bulbs into a medium baking dish and season with salt. Add the olive oil, Chicken Stock, lemon juice, vermouth, garlic, and thyme. Braise in the oven until fork tender, about 30 minutes. Serve the braised fennel immediately or let it cool in the cooking liquid and serve at room temperature.

CAVIAR D'AUBERGINE

Serves 6

2 medium eggplants, about 1 pound each

Juice of 2 lemons

2 cloves garlic, peeled

Leaves from 1 sprig fresh thyme

Pinch of red pepper

¼ cup plus 1 tablespoon olive oil

Salt

Freshly ground black pepper

1 cup cherry tomatoes, halved

Leaves from 1 sprig fresh basil

EGGPLANT CAVIAR IS USUALLY THOUGHT OF AS AN HORS D'OEUVRE, but I love to serve it as a side dish to anything from fish to lamb. In Provence, only a really excellent olive oil would be used for this eggplant purée, since a good, fruity oil perfectly complements the earthy flavor of eggplant.

1. Preheat the oven to 375° or prepare a hot grill. Place the eggplants directly on a rack and roast or grill until the skins are blistered and the eggplants are tender, almost collapsed, about 50 minutes. Let cool.

2. Peel away the eggplant skin and scoop the flesh into the bowl of a food processor. Add half of the lemon juice, the garlic, thyme, and red pepper. With the processor running, slowly add the ¼ cup olive oil

until the eggplant becomes a smooth purée. Scrape the eggplant into a medium bowl and season with salt and pepper. Cover and chill for at least 1 hour to let the flavors meld together.

3. Just before serving, toss the cherry tomatoes with the remaining lemon juice and 1 tablespoon olive oil and the basil. Spoon on top of the eggplant purée and serve at room temperature.

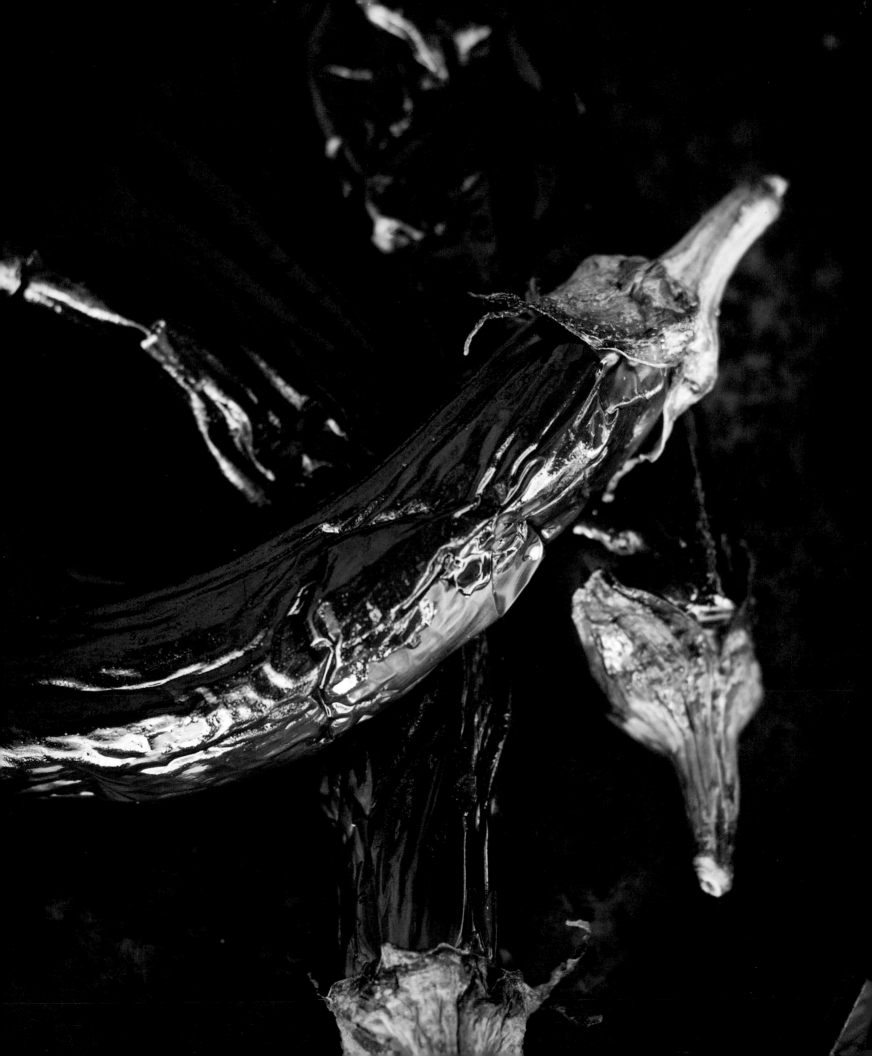

WHITE ASPARAGUS WITH POACHED EGG DRESSING

Serves 4

1 bunch white asparagus, about 1½ pounds

Salt

Juice of 1 lemon

2 tablespoons sugar

2 eggs, at room temperature

2 cloves garlic, coarsely chopped

1 small shallot, chopped

¼ cup verjus

½ cup olive oil

½ small bunch fresh chives, chopped

Leaves from 3 sprigs fresh tarragon, chopped

WHITE ASPARAGUS, ADORED IN BOTH THE BLACK FOREST AND PROVENCE, is found during its short season on haute cuisine menus as well as rustic ones. Don't confuse white asparagus with its green cousin, as it requires a lot more care. White spears must be cooked a little longer and at a lower temperature so that they lose their astringency and develop a sweet, delicate flavor. They're classically served with an egg-based dressing and thin slices of cured ham.

1. Trim about an inch from the ends of each asparagus spear, then peel with a vegetable peeler. Bring a large pot of salted water to a boil and add the lemon juice and sugar. Drop in the asparagus and simmer for about 10 minutes; drain.

2. Bring the eggs to a simmer in a small pot of water. Remove the pot from the heat and cover. Let sit for about 3 minutes, allowing the eggs to slowly cook. Crack the eggs into a blender, using a teaspoon to make sure you've removed all the egg from the shells.

3. Add the garlic, shallots, and *verjus* to the blender. Sprinkle with a bit of salt and blend. With the blender running, add the olive oil slowly, until everything is fully incorporated and the dressing is creamy and pale yellow. Pour the dressing into a small bowl. Fold in the chives and tarragon and season with salt. Serve the asparagus with the warm dressing.

AT THE MARKET in St-Rémy in 1994, I fell hard for asparagus in all colors, shapes, and sizes. Wouldn't you?

STUFFED ZUCCHINI BLOSSOMS WITH TOMATO VINAIGRETTE

Serves 6

1 cup fresh ricotta
cheese

Leaves from
2 sprigs fresh mint,
chopped

Leaves from
2 sprigs fresh basil,
chopped

1 clove garlic,
finely chopped

1 egg yolk

1 tablespoon fresh
bread crumbs

Salt

Freshly ground
black pepper

12 zucchini blossoms

1 cup flour, sifted

1 egg

Canola oil,
for frying

FOR THE TOMATO
VINAIGRETTE

1 small shallot,
chopped

1 tablespoon sherry
vinegar

¼ cup olive oil

1 pint cherry
tomatoes, halved

1 tablespoon finely
chopped fresh
chives

TO SERVE THESE CRISPY TREATS as an appetizer, I like to garnish a platter of them with some salad greens mixed with the Tomato Vinaigrette. It's perfectly fine to stuff the blossoms in advance, then refrigerate for up to an hour or two before battering and then frying them up at the very last minute.

1. In a medium bowl, mix together the ricotta, mint, basil, garlic, egg yolk, and bread crumbs. Season with salt and pepper. Put the cheese mixture in a piping bag (or in a small resealable plastic bag with a corner snipped off). Pipe the mixture into the zucchini blossoms. Refrigerate the filled blossoms for about 10 minutes.

2. Mix the batter in a large bowl by whisking together the flour, egg, and 1 cup ice water.

3. To fry the blossoms, heat about 4 inches of oil in a medium, heavy-bottomed saucepan until it reaches 350° on a candy thermometer. Dip the blossoms one at a time into the batter, then gently drop into the hot oil in batches. Fry, turning them from time to time, until golden brown, 1–2 minutes. Repeat until all the blossoms are fried. As they are done, drain on paper towels. Sprinkle with salt.

4. For the Vinaigrette, whisk together the shallots, vinegar, and olive oil in a small bowl. Toss with the tomatoes and chives and season with salt and pepper. Serve with the fried zucchini blossoms.

GRILLED PORCINI SALAD

Serves 6

1 pound fresh
porcini or other
wild mushrooms

Olive oil

Salt

Freshly ground
black pepper

1 tablespoon
sherry vinegar

1 green onion,
chopped

Leaves from
2 sprigs fresh basil

Parmesan for
grating

THIS VERY SIMPLE RECIPE enhances the incredible natural flavors of wild mushrooms. You can use any variety: matsutake, hen of the woods, and even wild oyster mushrooms achieve a new level of flavor from the heat of a wood-fired grill. Serve with young lettuces tossed with a simple vinaigrette.

1. Wipe away dirt from the mushrooms and scrape off any discolored patches from the stems. Cut the mushrooms in half and rub with a generous amount of olive oil, salt, and pepper.

2. Prepare a charcoal or gas grill, or heat a grill pan over high heat. Put the mushrooms directly on the grill and cook for 2–3 minutes on each side.

3. Transfer the mushrooms to a platter and drizzle with the vinegar, olive oil, and salt and pepper. Scatter green onions, basil leaves, and grate some Parmesan on top.

CRESPÉOU OF YARD EGGS, POTATOES & CHARD

Serves 6

4 tablespoons
olive oil

1 large Yukon Gold
or yellow potato,
cut into ¼-inch-
thick slices

Salt

2 cloves garlic,
crushed

Pinch of
red pepper flakes

1 bunch Swiss chard,
stems removed,
leaves washed and
chopped

12 eggs

Freshly ground
black pepper

THIS FRITTATA-LIKE OMELETTE is a classic in Provence, and use lots of the freshest eggs to bind the ingredients. From tomatoes to potatoes, all sorts of vegetables can find their way into this little torta. My Provence-born chef Chris would make them with just about any leftovers. I serve Crespéou hot or cold, depending on the weather and my mood.

1. Preheat the oven to 350°. Heat 2 tablespoons of the olive oil in a large, ovenproof skillet over medium-high heat. Add the potatoes and sauté until browned on both sides, about 10 minutes. Remove the potatoes with a slotted spoon and drain on paper towels. Sprinkle with salt.

2. To the same skillet, add the garlic, pepper flakes, and Swiss chard and cook until the leaves are wilted, about 2 minutes. In a large bowl, whisk together the eggs and season with salt and pepper. Add the wilted Swiss chard and potatoes.

3. Heat the remaining 2 tablespoons olive oil in the same skillet over high heat. Add the eggs, a bit at a time, and stir the mixture for a minute in the hot skillet. Transfer the skillet to the oven and bake for 10–12 minutes, or until the eggs have set. Cut into wedges and serve right from the pan.

PUMPKIN TIAN

Serves 6-8

1 4–5-pound sweet pumpkin or Kabocha squash

3 tablespoons olive oil

2 cloves garlic, sliced

1 sprig fresh thyme

Dash of cayenne pepper

Dash of nutmeg

Salt

Freshly ground black pepper

4 eggs

1 cup cream

¼ cup grated Parmesan cheese

I'M SO PLEASED by the presentation of this tian, where the shell of the squash becomes the baking and serving vessel that you bring to the table. If you don't want to bother with the shell, you can bake the scooped out pumpkin and custard in a shallow casserole.

1. Preheat the oven to 325°. Cut the top off the pumpkin, about 3 inches below the stem, and reserve to serve with the squash. With a spoon, scoop out the seeds. (You can roast the pumpkin seeds for a nice snack: toss the cleaned seeds in olive oil and a pinch of salt, spread on a baking pan, and roast in a 350° oven for 15–20 minutes, until golden brown.) Use a spoon to scrape out as much of the pumpkin as you can, leaving the shell intact. Chop the flesh.

2. Heat the olive oil in a large skillet over medium-high. Add the garlic and pumpkin flesh and cook, stirring occasionally, until the pumpkin is tender, about 10 minutes. Add the thyme, cayenne, and nutmeg and season with salt and pepper. Spoon the sautéed pumpkin back into the shell.

3. In a small bowl, whisk together the eggs, cream, and Parmesan and pour into the pumpkin shell. Place on a baking pan and bake until the top is golden brown and the custard is set, 45 minutes to 1 hour. Serve right from the pumpkin while it's still hot.

Anchovies &

CHAPTER SEVEN

Orange Peels

ORN IN THE
volatile times of 1927 to a world on the brink of the
Great Depression, Constantin Kerageorgiou, of
Greek ancestry, was raised French in the tiny
Mediterranean village of Port-Saint-Louis. Provençal
to the core, his smile was grand and his dramatic
flair made him a sight to behold whenever he had
an audience. That's precisely why he was drawn to
the restaurant business, or why it was drawn to him.
Passion ran through his veins, how could it not?
He was both Greek *and* French. His personality
was far greater than his stature. Chris towered all of
five-feet-three, but he was barrel-chested and strong
as a mule. Driven by the passions of his heritage, he
loved me *and* often hated me—sometimes both in
the same day.

**OUR HOUSE IN PROVENCE, left, at least for a week. Blue shutters, old
stone, airy courtyards, a kitchen to cook in. Overleaf, I learned the essence
of deep, authentic Provençal flavor from my Chef Chris.**

163

"Chef Chris was Provençal to the core. Driven by the passions of his heritage, he often loved me and hated me, sometimes in the same day."

Chris's kitchen at La Provence in Lacombe, Louisiana, was his perfectly imperfect little world, and by that I mean it was made perfect through his spontaneous imperfection. Just like his cooking, the restaurant wasn't great because of his finesse

but because of his love. Love not only for what he was cooking, but for the life he lived and the people who lived in his world. Certainly his guests were the most beloved, second only to the dogs that roamed the kitchen as he cooked. The staff he surrounded himself with were special—people whom he had saved and others, who, some would say, saved him. Chris had a real soft spot for helping people, perhaps because he was never far from a childhood during the German Occupation that led him to join the Résistance, the French Underground, at the age of 14. He always saw himself as the poor but proud little boy who had to fight for everything he had, and that attitude shaped his cooking with a style that would leave its indelible imprint on me.

Chris came to America in 1947 as a baker on a big ocean liner; we were lucky that he decided to jump that ship in New Orleans. He spent a career making relationships and forging a defining path, creating a French *auberge* deep in the countryside on the north shore of Lake Pontchartrain, a long causeway away from New Orleans. He never heard of the word *locavore,* but he was a true believer, not because a fad or trend or a glossy periodical told him to think that way. It just made sense to Chris to

form relationships with folks in his neck in the woods, honoring those local farmers, fishermen, and foragers with his business. His menu was a highly personal mix of what was in season and the flavors of his childhood. For years he had his mother in the kitchen and she'd make her repertoire: daubes, *estouffades, caillettes,* and *pieds et paquets.* Dishes so typically Provençal, so old and yet so way before their time. Chris Kerageorgiou is still regarded today as one of the best New Orleans chefs ever.

I grew up on Bayou Liberty, two bayous away from Chef Chris's Bayou Lacombe. Attracted by the mystique of the half-crazy, half-genius chef, customers were drawn to La Provence in hopes of catching a glimpse of him as he slammed pots and pans around the kitchen, freely cursing in at least one other language. He was drama just waiting to happen.

CHEF CHRIS at La Provence in 1995. Photo: David Grunfeld.

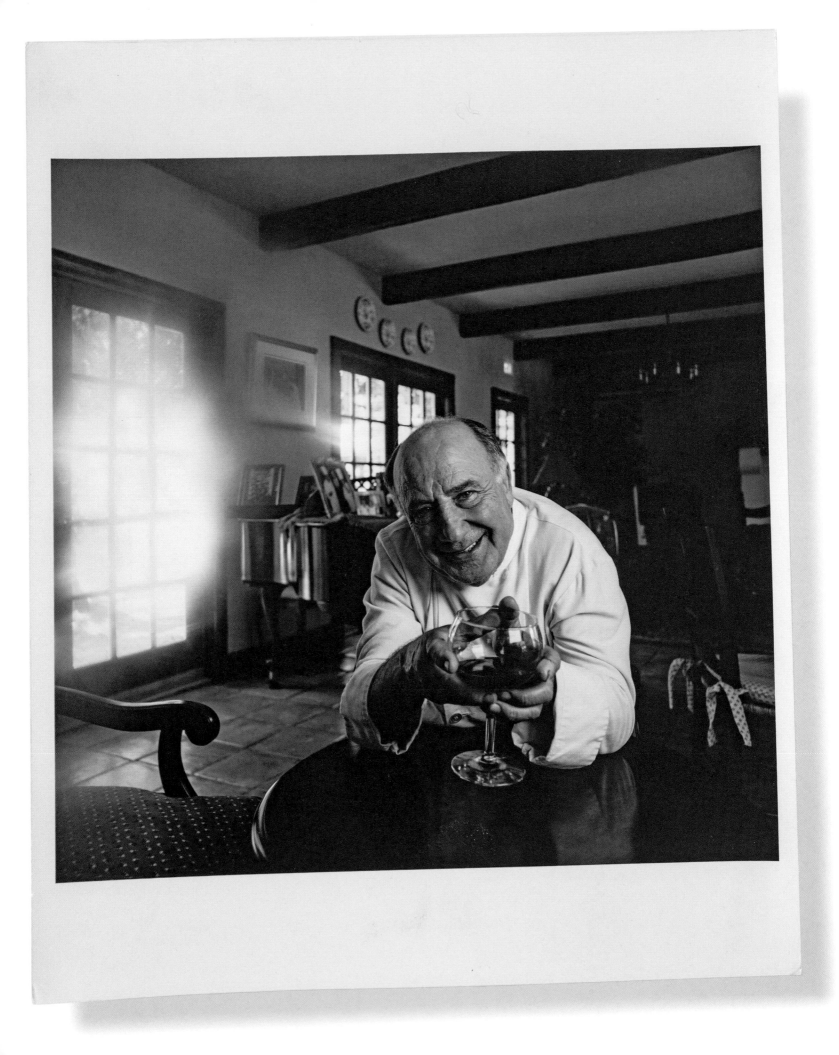

DRIED SAUSAGES, the famed *saucissons sec* of France, in a fine display at the Apt market, above. Sliced for hors d'oeuvres, left. At La Provence, 1996 in Lacombe, LA, with Chef Chris, above right. Chris's cookbook.

This was my Chef Chris, my second mentor who truly taught me how to love each and every guest through the food we made for them. The same Chef Chris who taught me to break rules and to be true to the soul of grand cuisine, even if we had no foie gras and no truffles. He believed that if you use simple ingredients, handle them with love and care, the results will exceed the efforts of other cooks whose dependence on rich and luxurious ingredients limits their creativity. Some chefs of that era wasted much in the kitchen in their efforts to create great food, but not Chris. Never far from that poor child in Provence, Chris wasted nothing. When he juiced an orange, he always made certain that the peels were saved, hung, and dried to flavor his braises and stews. The same could be said for nearly everything he touched. As he cracked eggs, he would use his stubby little thumbs to remove every ounce of egg white from the shell, swearing that by doing so he'd get an extra egg from every dozen. Those eggshells would then go to feed his beloved roses. Never quite adjusting to the comforts and excesses of his adopted home, his spice cabinets were not filled with frivolous blends but rather depended upon sea salt, crushed red pepper flakes, black pepper, curing salt, dried bay leaves and thyme, Quatre Épices Bovida, gorgeous olive oils, sherry vinegar, and anchovies. Simplicity was his mark and in many ways he passed that on to me.

166

"*I was to go to Chris's Provence, to taste what he tasted, to shop his hometown markets, to know his butchers. In short, I was to learn to cook and eat like a Provençal.*"

Cooking With

Chris and Goffredo
Louisiana and Mediterranean Cuisine

A particularly great example was his way of braising a lamb shoulder using a few minced anchovies and the orange peel that would bring out sweet subtle flavors of the lamb. Neither the anchovies nor the orange peel could be detected after hours of slow cooking, but they made all the difference (see the recipe on page 171). "Listen Baby, dis is how ma mamma did it, it's *la vraie*. The real way! They don' teach you in culinary ecole." Or, "Just like the aïoli, de recipe is all ways one garlic clove per person an' you can't use da machine, it mus' be from hand, you have to earn it, Baby, with da mortar an' da pedestal."

Set in his ways, Chris never fully trusted me to cook his heirloom Provençal family recipes. And I don't blame him. I find myself following his moves exactly today when cooking Chris's food. I'll never forget pushing him over the edge one time when I made a batch of ratatouille. With all of the vegetables perfectly diced and cooked down to the desired consistency while carefully retaining the color of the peppers, zucchini, and squash, I thought I'd exercise a little artistic free-

dom by adding minced mint as opposed to basil. The result, or so I thought, was another stroke of John Besh genius. I brought him a healthy spoonful, eager for his coronation, and he damn near decapitated me with the chair that he threw. He cursed me in seven languages, his eyes dramatically closed while looking toward the ceiling with outspread arms. Clearly, his ratatouille was more important to him than it was to me. He made his point and what a point he did make. I'm not sure if he fired me that day, as I couldn't fully understand much of what he was saying. I was, in fact, often told to leave his kitchen for good. Normally, I'd return to work the next day as if nothing had happened and once he was able to fully accept the fact that I had not altered his recipe out of malice, he would forgive me and we could move on.

On this particular day, he decided he'd remedy my ignorance once and for all by sending me to learn in Provence. Not the Provence that I knew through the holidays I took while living and cooking in Germany, but *his* Provence. I was to taste what he tasted. Learn what he learned—from his hometown markets and butchers and favorite restaurants. In short, I was to learn how to cook and eat like a Provençal. Only after several summers in France—with Chris, his family, and friends who we'd cook with, drink with, and learn from—would I be allowed to prepare his gutsy food. And it was only after this journey that I could fully appreciate those anchovies and orange peels. Food is much more than sustenance or a body of recipes. It was for Chris an expression of a culture, of friends and family. Food is that thread we all have in common that shapes us and nourishes our spirit. I had to not only understand his people to cook his food, but I had to love his people to cook with integrity.

RAGOUT OF LAMB SHOULDER WITH CAVATELLI

Serves 6–8

¼ cup olive oil

1 5-pound bone-in lamb shoulder

1 teaspoon fennel seeds, crushed

Leaves from 1 sprig fresh rosemary, chopped

Salt

Freshly ground black pepper

1 bunch leeks, trimmed, chopped, and cleaned

1 stalk celery, chopped

4 cloves garlic, chopped

Pinch red pepper flakes

3 filets salt-cured anchovies

2 tablespoons tomato paste

Leaves from 4 sprigs fresh thyme, chopped

1 bay leaf

1½ cups red wine

Peel of ½ orange

1 cup red pearl onions, peeled

2 cups Basic Fond de Veau (page 121)

1 16-ounce package cavatelli pasta, cooked

1 cup fresh sweet peas

AT FIRST GLANCE, this might look like a simple lamb stew, but you will be delighted by its finesse when you remove the lamb from the bone, return it to the pot, and toss with your favorite pasta. The secret to this deep and succulent sauce is the Fond de Veau (page 121), a reduced veal stock whose unctuousness is well worth the extra preparation. The lamb can be made ahead, to concentrate the flavors. This ragout makes a surprisingly satisfying dish for entertaining.

1. Heat the oil in a large, heavy-bottomed pot over high heat. Season the lamb shoulder with the fennel, rosemary, salt, and pepper. Add the lamb to the pot and sear on all sides, turning occasionally, until golden brown, 5–7 minutes. Transfer to a platter.

2. Add the leeks, celery, garlic, and red pepper flakes to the pot and cook until softened, about 5 minutes. Add the anchovies, tomato paste, thyme, and bay leaf and cook, stirring constantly, until a dark, mahogany-colored crust forms on the bottom of the pot, 3–4 minutes.

3. Add the wine and bring to a boil, stirring constantly. Return the lamb to the pot and add the orange peel, red onions, and Fond de Veau. Cover and bring to a boil. Reduce the heat to a slow simmer and cook until the lamb is tender, about 2 hours. Remove from the heat and let the lamb cool in the pot, covered. Discard the bay leaf.

4. When you're ready to serve, pull the lamb meat from the bone and return to the rich sauce in the pot along with the cooked pasta. Add the sweet peas and warm thoroughly before serving.

PROVENÇAL ROAST LEG OF LAMB

Serves 6–8

1 6-pound bone-in
leg of lamb

¼ cup olive oil

Zest of 1 lemon

Leaves from 8
sprigs fresh thyme

Salt

Freshly ground
black pepper

6 cloves garlic,
thinly sliced

2 long branches
fresh rosemary

IF YOU FIND A BONELESS LEG OF LAMB instead of a bone-in leg, this roast will work perfectly fine. It's really about the quality of the lamb and letting its flavor come through. A farm-raised lamb from your farmers market will be so much more succulent and delicious than the mass-produced alternative.

1. Preheat the oven to 375°. Truss the lamb with butcher's twine.

2. Rub the lamb with the olive oil and season with the lemon zest, thyme, salt, and pepper. With a small knife, make tiny slits all over the surface of the lamb and insert a slice of garlic and a sprig of rosemary into each.

3. Put a rack in a roasting pan and place the lamb on top. Roast the lamb until it registers 130° on a meat thermometer, 45–60 minutes.

BUTCHER SHOP CHICKEN WITH HERBES DE PROVENCE

Serves 4

1 3-4-pound organic
chicken

3 tablespoons
olive oil

2 tablespoons herbes
de Provence

Salt

Freshly ground
black pepper

HERE'S HOW I THINK ABOUT HERBES DE PROVENCE: Sure, the real thing is always better. If you can get your hands on fresh thyme, rosemary, marjoram, and lavender, wonderful. But sometimes you just can't. And for those sometimes, the packaged dried herbs will do just fine, especially on a roast chicken. Outside of every Provençal butcher shop and in many markets, chickens rubbed with dried herbs are roasting on rotisseries, and they taste wonderful.

1. Preheat the oven to 400°. Rub the chicken with the olive oil and season with the herbes de Provence, salt, and pepper. Place in a roasting pan on a rack and roast until the skin is golden brown and the juices run clear when pricked, 40–45 minutes.

CHEF CHRIS'S ARTICHOKES BARIGOULE

Serves 6

6 large artichokes

6 tablespoons olive oil

1 leek, cleaned and chopped

4 cloves garlic, chopped

2 filets salt-cured anchovies

½ cup chopped cured ham (such as prosciutto)

2 cups wild mushrooms, chopped

Pinch red pepper flakes

1 bay leaf

Leaves from 1 sprig fresh thyme

Leaves from 1 sprig fresh savory

¼ cup chopped tomatoes

½ cup fresh bread crumbs

Salt

Freshly ground black pepper

1½ cups dry white wine

2 cups Basic Chicken Stock (page 250)

THESE BRAISED STUFFED ARTICHOKES were what my mentor grew up eating for dinner, when meager end pieces of ham, stale bread, and a few wild mushrooms would turn simple artichokes into a whole meal. Named for the *barigoulo,* the Provençal word for morel-like mushrooms, I often serve Artichokes Barigoule as a hearty appetizer or even as the main dish at lunch with a salad. It's so much easier to scoop out the pesky choke after the artichokes have been briefly blanched.

1. To prepare the artichokes, trim off the thorny leaves from the bottom of each and cut off the top third of the bulb. Briefly blanch the artichokes in boiling salted water so that the stems just begin to soften, about 10 minutes. Drain and let cool. With a spoon, scoop out the fuzzy choke.

2. Make the stuffing by heating 3 tablespoons of the olive oil in a large, heavy-bottomed pot over medium-high heat. Add the leeks, garlic, and anchovies and cook until the onions and leeks are softened and the anchovies have melted into the oil, about 5 minutes. Add the ham, mushrooms, red pepper, bay leaf, thyme, and savory and cook until the ham is slightly browned, 4–5 minutes. Turn off the heat and stir in the tomatoes and bread crumbs. Discard the bay leaf. Season with salt and pepper.

3. Scoop the stuffing mixture into the artichokes. Heat the remaining 3 tablespoons olive oil in the large pot over medium-high heat. Add the stuffed artichokes, wine, and Chicken Stock. Cover and simmer, turning once, until the artichokes are tender, about 1 hour. Serve hot or at room temperature.

SLOW-COOKED RABBIT WITH CREAMY ROSEMARY TURNIPS

Serves 4

¼ cup olive oil

1 4-pound young rabbit, quartered

Salt

Freshly ground black pepper

1 onion, chopped

1 carrot, peeled and chopped

1 stalk celery, chopped

2 cloves garlic, sliced

2 cups wild mushrooms, chopped

1 tablespoon tomato paste

1 bay leaf

2 sprigs fresh thyme

½ cup dry white wine

4 cups Basic Chicken Stock (page 250)

4 small purple turnips, peeled and quartered

1 Yukon Gold potato, peeled and quartered

1 sprig fresh rosemary

4 tablespoons butter

THINK OF SERVING THE CREAMY turnips like mashed potatoes with gravy. Chicken legs and thighs, or other fowl like pheasant, make perfect substitutes in this stew.

1. Heat the oil in a large, heavy-bottomed pot over medium-high heat. Season the rabbit with salt and pepper and sear in the hot oil until all sides are golden brown, 10–15 minutes. Transfer to a platter.

2. Add the onions, carrots, celery, and garlic to the pot and cook until browned, about 8 minutes. Add the mushrooms, tomato paste, bay leaf, and thyme and cook, stirring constantly, for about 5 minutes.

3. Add the white wine and Chicken Stock, bring to a boil, and stir well. Return the rabbit to the pot and cover. Reduce the heat and simmer until the rabbit meat is soft and tender, about 1 hour. Remove the rabbit from the pot.

4. Raise the heat to medium high and simmer until the cooking liquid is reduced by half, to about 2½ cups, 15–20 minutes. Just before serving, pull the meat from the bones, and drop it back into the sauce. Discard the bay leaf and thyme sprigs.

5. Meanwhile, put the turnips, potato, and rosemary in a medium saucepan, cover with water, and season with salt. Bring to a boil over high heat. Reduce the heat and simmer until tender, 20–25 minutes. Drain, and discard the rosemary. Put the turnips, potatoes, and butter into a food processor and blend (or mash with a potato-masher) into a smooth purée. Season with salt and pepper and serve.

DAUBE OF BEEF PROVENÇAL

Serves 6–8

¼ cup olive oil

3 pounds beef chuck, cut into 2-inch chunks

1 tablespoon herbes de Provence

Salt

Freshly ground black pepper

1 medium onion, chopped

1 stalk celery, chopped

1 carrot, peeled and chopped

4 cloves garlic, peeled and crushed

2 filets salt-cured anchovies

2 tablespoons tomato paste

1½ cups red wine

Peel of ½ orange

1 bay leaf

1 sprig fresh rosemary

3 cups Basic Fond de Veau (page 121)

I LEARNED THIS SLOW-COOKED STEW from the frugal Chef Chris who would typically make a daube from almost any lesser cut of beef, lamb, goat, or pork. The lesser cuts are the muscles that are often tougher—but tastier—so a long braise in wine and a rich veal stock makes them tender and more flavorful, too. The luxurious Fond de Veau (page 121) works its magic here. Serve the daube with rice or your favorite pasta to sop up the rich juices.

1. Heat the oil in a large, heavy-bottomed pot over high heat. Season the beef with the herbes de Provence, salt, and pepper. In batches, add the beef to the hot oil and sear until all sides are golden brown, transferring the browned pieces to a platter as you work.

2. Add the onions, celery, carrot, garlic, and anchovies to the pot and cook, stirring, until the vegetables are caramelized, about 6 minutes. Add the tomato paste and cook, stirring constantly, until it becomes a dark, mahogany color, 3–4 minutes. Add the wine, orange peel, bay leaf, rosemary, and Fond de Veau. Return the beef to the pot, cover, and simmer for about 1 hour. Uncover the pot and continue to simmer for another 30 minutes, until the beef is very tender. Discard the bay leaf and rosemary and serve.

175

SLOW-COOKED TENDER TRIPE

Serves 8

2 pounds tripe

Salt

8 lemons

3 cups white vinegar

¼ cup olive oil

1 large onion, chopped

1 carrot, peeled and chopped

1 stalk celery, chopped

1 teaspoon crushed coriander

1 teaspoon Aleppo pepper or crushed red pepper flakes

1 teaspoon herbes de Provence

3 cups Cherry Tomato Five-Minute Sauce (opposite) or crushed canned tomatoes

1 cup Basic Fond de Veau (page 121)

1 teaspoon grated lemon zest

1 sprig fresh rosemary

1 bay leaf

Freshly ground black pepper

1 16-ounce package garganelli or other short tube pasta, cooked

Parmesan cheese for grating

Leaves from 4 sprigs fresh basil, thinly sliced

THE RECIPE FOR THIS GUTSY, MARSEILLE-STYLE tripe ragout in a rich aromatic, tomato gravy comes directly from Chris's mother who lived in Port-St.-Louis. The tripe acts as a sponge absorbing all the intense flavors. I was never a fan of tripe until I had Chris's version; he'd make it to serve to his favorite friends or even sometimes, on special occasions, for family meal at La Provence. In Provence itself, hearty ragouts like this one are revered and served on feast days. A note in advance: Chris soaked his tripe for 2 days before cooking and so do I.

1. To thoroughly clean the tripe, soak in a bowl of salted water with the juice of 4 lemons and refrigerate overnight. Drain and repeat for another day.

2. Bring a large pot of salted water to a boil and add 1 cup vinegar and the tripe. Blanch the tripe for about 10 minutes; drain in a colander. Repeat this blanching step twice. Transfer the tripe to a board and cut into thin strips.

3. Heat the oil in a large, heavy-bottomed pot over medium-high heat. Add the onions, carrots, celery, coriander, Aleppo pepper, and herbes de Provence. Cook until browned and softened, 5–7 minutes.

4. Add the tripe, tomato sauce, Fond de Veau, lemon zest, rosemary, and bay leaf and bring to a boil. Reduce the heat, cover, and simmer until the tripe is tender, about 1 hour. Season with salt and pepper. Discard the rosemary sprig and bay leaf.

5. To serve, toss the tripe with the cooked pasta and sprinkle with the Parmesan and basil.

CHERRY TOMATO FIVE-MINUTE SAUCE

Makes 1½ quarts

¼ cup olive oil

2 quarts ripe cherry tomatoes, halved

2 teaspoons crushed red pepper flakes

4 cloves garlic, peeled and crushed

Leaves from 4 sprigs fresh basil

Salt

Freshly ground black pepper

THIS IS MY FAVORITE QUICK, BRIGHT TOMATO SAUCE, and even though I've included this recipe in my two previous books, I give it to you again, because using it makes such a difference in the flavor of any dish.

1. Heat the oil in a large saucepan over high heat. Add the tomatoes, pepper flakes, and garlic and bring to a boil. Reduce the heat to medium and cook, stirring occasionally with a wooden spoon, for another 5 minutes. Add the basil.

2. Pour the sauce into a food mill and purée. Season with salt and pepper. If you're not using it immediately, transfer the sauce to resealable plastic bags or quart containers and freeze.

BRANDADE DE MORUE AU GRATIN

Serves 6–8

1 pound dried
salt cod

2 Yukon Gold or
yellow potatoes,
peeled and
quartered

4 cloves garlic,
peeled and crushed

1 sprig fresh thyme

1 cup plus
1 tablespoon
olive oil

Pinch of *piment
d'Espelette* or
cayenne pepper

Juice of 1 lemon

Salt

Freshly ground
black pepper

½ cup fresh bread
crumbs

½ cup grated
Parmesan cheese

IN THIS PROVENÇAL CLASSIC, salt cod is puréed with potatoes, then topped with bread crumbs and cheese at the last minute and baked. Sometimes it's difficult to look at a dry slab of salt cod and imagine a succulent dish, but soaking it does work magic. After its overnight bath, the cod reemerges as a soft, white, flaky fish just waiting to be cooked in any number of ways.

1. Rinse the salt cod under cold water and soak in a bowl of water in the refrigerator overnight, changing the water twice.

2. Preheat the oven to 400°. Cut the cod into smaller pieces and combine with the potatoes, garlic, and thyme in a medium pot. Cover with cold water and bring to a boil over high heat. Reduce the heat to medium and simmer until the cod and potatoes are tender, 15–20 minutes. Discard the thyme and drain.

3. Put the cod and potatoes in a food processor. With the processor running, add the 1 cup olive oil until you have a shiny, smooth purée. Season with the *piment d'Espelette*, lemon juice, salt, and pepper.

4. Spoon the purée into a baking dish. Stir together the bread crumbs, cheese, and remaining 1 tablespoon oil and sprinkle on top. Bake until the bread crumbs are golden brown, about 25 minutes. Serve hot with crusty bread.

SALT COD FRITTERS

THIS IS A DELIGHTFUL LITTLE TREAT to make with leftover Brandade. Just save some of the mix before you add the topping. Chill the Brandade overnight. Heat 4 inches canola oil in a small, heavy-bottomed pot until it reaches 350° on a candy thermometer. In a large bowl, whisk together 1 cup flour, 1 cup ice water, and 1 egg until smooth. Wet your hands and scoop 1-inch balls from the purée, rolling each between your palms. Dip each ball into the batter, then drop into the hot oil, a few at a time. Fry until golden brown, 3–5 minutes. Drain on paper towels, sprinkle with salt, and serve while still hot.

ALAIN'S GRAND AÏOLI WITH COD

Serves 6

FOR THE COD & VEGETABLES

2 quarts Basic Fish Stock (page 40)

3 stalks fresh or dried fennel

2 leeks, cleaned and chopped

3 bay leaves

Salt

Freshly ground black pepper

3 medium artichokes, halved, chokes removed

6 medium red beets, peeled and quartered

6 small yellow potatoes

1 small head cauliflower, cut into florets

½ pound string beans

1½ pounds fresh cod, cut into 4–6-ounce portions

18 sea snails (optional)

FOR THE AÏOLI

2 egg yolks

6 cloves garlic, peeled

Juice of ½ lemon

2 cups olive oil

Salt

Freshly ground black pepper

AÏOLI IS THE HEAVENLY signature sauce of Provence, an homage to fresh garlic and the best olive oil. At his restaurant in St.-Rémy-de-Provence, Alain Assaud serves this Grand Aïoli as a momentous but casual Sunday afternoon supper, where it's eaten in a communal way: platters of vegetables, snails, poached fish, whatever, are placed in the center of a big table to be topped with his Aïoli, which he makes by hand in his ancient olivewood mortar and pestle. The idea is to steam or poach the vegetables and seafood in a flavorful broth, and then to dip them in the Aïoli.

1. To steam the cod and vegetables, in a large pot, bring the Fish Stock, fennel, leeks, bay leaves, salt, and pepper to a boil over medium-high heat. Insert a steamer basket or colander. Add the artichokes, beets, and potatoes. Cover and steam them until tender, about 25 minutes. Transfer to a large platter. Add cauliflower and green beans, cover and steam until tender, about 10 minutes. Transfer to the platter.

2. Add 1 quart water to the pot and return the fragrant broth to a boil. Add the cod to the broth and cook for 5 minutes. Add the sea snails if using, cover, and simmer for another 3 minutes. Remove the cod and snails to the platter.

3. For the Aïoli, combine the yolks, garlic, and lemon juice in the bowl of a food processor. Pulse until the garlic cloves are chopped. With the processor running, add the olive oil in a steady stream until it becomes a shiny sauce. Season with salt and pepper. Serve the Aïoli with the steamed vegetables and cod.

Mussel Madness in Marseille

W

HILE I WAS cooking for Chef Chris Kerageorgiou in 1995 at La Provence in Lacombe, Louisiana, I was given a chance to understand Provence in ways I'd never imagined. At this point in my life, I did think I knew a little something about French cooking. But not according to Chef Chris, who decided to send me to spend time with his family near the port city of Marseille to truly experience the roots of Provençal cooking. Learning a cuisine from books is one thing. Learning traditional food from home cooks is a completely different story. I've always been surprised by how many French chefs never appreciate the value of understanding the old ways of their own people. That same year, I arrived in Marseille with my brother Steve, an oncologist from

I LOVE TO CELEBRATE the bounty of local shellfish by serving it up in great bowls and platters with crusty bread, left. Overleaf, Mussels on the Half Shell with lemon and lots of pastis.

185

MARSEILLE as I knew it in 1996, above. Fisherman at the Vieux Port in the 1950s, right. The mussel scene in Marseille today, far right.

Memphis, at the docks of Port-Saint-Louis, where we met up with Chris's cousin Pierre, a dramatic local as wide as he was tall and whose eyes danced with mischief. That guy was smart and clever at the same time. His plan: to teach us "how to make the *moules*." I had no idea what that would entail, but sensed it could be interesting. Cousin Pierre and a guy who seemed to be either a mob boss, a union heavy, or both, started walking us along the docks of Marseille to meet up with Pierre's son, who had some wine for us. That wine, as it turned out, was just about to be shipped to Japan. However, since this was *French* wine, these Frenchmen decided they'd just keep a palette for themselves. For the sake of national pride, of course.

We loaded the wine onto a truck to be driven to the *locale municipale,* the equivalent of a union hall, just a few blocks from the docks. Then we were off to collect the *moules,* about 50 pounds of them, from another friend, who had just happened to acquire them from some unknown source, likely from a private piece of beach-front property posted by a rival mussel harvester. These turned out to be the famed Bouzigues mussels from farther west along the Mediterranean coast. This arrangement was not unlike our oyster leases in the marshes of South Louisiana. Even the coastline of the Camargue resembled ours, with expansive salt marsh estuaries on one side of the highway and rice fields on the other. The "making of the *moules*" hadn't even begun, but I was already learning something about these Frenchmen, how like my people of Louisiana they are!

"Dozens of workers lined up at the door: a dock 'strike' had been called to celebrate the visitors from Nouvelle Orléans."

hall, large propane burners were brought out and fitted with three crawfish boil–size pots, the flames lit, and large jugfuls of olive oil drizzled in. Trying to decipher their thick Provençal dialect, I understood that this was the finest olive oil produced in France. Since it, too, had been destined to be shipped off to some other country, my new friends were only doing their national duty to rescue some of it for La Belle France.

As the oil began to heat, we were up to our elbows in a large industrial sink, scrubbing each and every *moule,* removing each and every beard until they all shone. Even though I'd done this many, many times before, it seemed only right that they had to teach me their way. We tossed about a third of the mussels into one of the large pots along with at least one clove of garlic per person, sliced paper thin—there were pounds and pounds of garlic— and several minced shallots. A bottle or two of vermouth was poured in, until the liquid nearly covered the *moules,* then a handful of dried and crushed red chiles—*piments forts*—that could have been our cayenne, and a couple of branches of fresh thyme. In about 10 minutes, the *moules* began to open. Since Pierre ran everything, he ran the

We just can't help ourselves: it's in our blood. Witnessing the way Pierre and his friends maneuvered felt like reading the *Times-Picayune*'s reports on the doings of our mischievous local politicians. We aren't more corrupt than anyone else, just a little more tolerant of it.

Once we returned to the *locale municipale,* it seems that every man of working age, dozens of them, was lined up at the door, waiting to be let in. Apparently a "strike" had been called on the docks to celebrate the visitors from Nouvelle Orléans and the teaching of the "making of the *moules*." Once we entered the gym-size meeting

MARSEILLE

tasting, too. Using an empty hinged mussel shell as a tongs, he began removing the mussels and handing them to me, just to make sure I knew how a real mussel should taste. And these mussels were different, with a brininess I'd never experienced. Salty, plump, and heavy, each mussel was surely a mouthful.

As we worked around our pot, another team of men began filling another huge pot with chopped tomatoes, garlic, onion, olive oil; then came the second batch of mussels and then minced basil, parsley, and thyme. That pot was allowed to come to a boil, the heat was lowered, the pot covered, and we waited another 15 minutes for the mussels to open. In the meantime, the last third of the *moules* had been shucked, left on the half shell and placed on platters of ice ready to be seasoned with white wine vinegar from random screw-top wine bottles with a hole punched in their top. All the while, at an incredible rate, the men were pouring pastis into glasses,

VINTAGE MARSEILLE, above. All that remains of a feast of mussels, clams, and snails, right.

which were then filled with ice water, turning it a signature milky green. I've never had so much Ricard in my life, nor did I ever consume so many mussels, both raw and cooked. At one point, I looked down at Steve, who had never eaten a raw mussel—or drunk pastis, for that matter. I watched him take one shot of pastis for every *moule* he put in his mouth, trying to polish off everything that was fed to him and to save face at the same time. I should have known he was drunk when the line of men suddenly shifted from the *moules,* pastis, and wine to Steve himself. Word had evidently gotten around that he was a doctor, and the men began to line up, 10 and 15 deep, to be diagnosed for some disease or other. One by one, those short, stocky dock workers began taking off their clothes to show Steve a scar, or wound, or infection. That's when I noticed my brother (who treats cancer patients) had started smoking Gauloises. The only problem was he was smoking the cigarettes backwards, lighting up the filtered end. To this day whenever I smell pastis and cigarettes I think of my brother and the best mussels in the world.

MUSSELS ON THE HALF SHELL

Serves 6

3 pounds mussels

2 lemons, sliced

Coarse sea salt

IN THIS COUNTRY, MOST OF OUR MUSSELS come from Prince Edward Island, Canada, so—probably because they're not local—we're not used to eating them raw. But along the Mediterranean Coast this is one of the most common and best ways to eat super-fresh mussels. Often aïoli is served alongside, but when you have the option of a mussel straight from the sea, it needs nothing more than a squeeze of lemon. Even lightly poached in white wine, they're wonderful on the half shell.

1. Rinse and scrub the mussels under cold running water and debeard them by pulling off their hanging threads. Discard any cracked mussels.

2. To shuck, hold a mussel with a folded kitchen towel, with the hinged end pointing away from you. Insert a pointed oyster knife about ¼ inch from the hinge and just wiggle the knife until the shell pops open. Gently run the knife under the mussel to loosen it, but keep it in the shell. Discard the top shell.

3. Arrange the shucked mussels on a large platter with the lemons and sea salt.

IMAGINE my delight at finding Bouzigues mussels from Chef Chris's hometown of Port-St.-Louis still being sold in Marseille today, left.

MOULES GRATINÉ

Serves 6

3 pounds mussels

4 tablespoons olive oil

1 shallot, chopped

1 clove garlic, chopped

1 cup vermouth

2 slices white country bread, toasted

2 ounces Parmesan cheese

3 green onions, green parts, thinly sliced

Leaves from 3 sprigs fresh parsley, chopped

Leaves from 2 sprigs fresh thyme

Salt

I LIKE TO MAKE A CRISPY CASSEROLE of these delectable mussels and bring it right from the oven to my waiting guests as they sip bright, cold glasses of white wine. With a bunch of forks to spear the mussels, and toasts to catch their delicious juices, this is a splendid first course.

1. Place a rack on the top shelf of the oven and preheat the broiler. Rinse and scrub the mussels under cold running water and debeard them by pulling off their hanging threads. Discard any cracked mussels.

2. Heat 2 tablespoons of the olive oil in a large, heavy-bottomed pot over medium-high heat. Add the shallots and garlic and cook until softened, 2–3 minutes. Deglaze the pot with the vermouth and bring to a boil. Add the mussels, cover, and steam just until they open, about 2 minutes. Drain in a colander, reserving the liquid, then spread the mussels on a baking sheet to cool.

3. Transfer the poaching liquid to a 3-quart baking dish. Pop the mussels from their shells and spread in a single layer on the bottom of the dish.

4. Using a box grater, grate the toasted bread along with the Parmesan cheese into a small bowl. You should have

about 1½ cups. Stir in the green onions, parsley, thyme, and the remaining 2 tablespoons olive oil. Season with salt. The mixture should be dry and not clumpy.

5. Top the mussels with the bread crumb mixture and place under the broiler. Broil until the bread crumbs are golden brown and crispy, about 5 minutes. Serve hot.

MOULES MARINIÈRE

Serves 6

4 pounds mussels

3 tablespoons olive oil

1 leek, rinsed and thinly sliced

2 green onions, thinly sliced

4 cloves garlic, chopped

1 cup vermouth

2 sprigs fresh thyme

2 sprigs fresh parsley

Salt

Freshly ground black pepper

AT FIRST GLANCE, this recipe seems so simple that you might wonder: "What am I dipping my bread into?" But as they open, the mussels release their tangy liquor into the vermouth, creating an aromatic broth worthy of bathing in!

1. Rinse and scrub the mussels under cold running water and debeard them by pulling off their hanging threads. Discard any cracked mussels.

2. Heat the oil in a large, heavy-bottomed pot over medium-high heat. Add the leeks, green onions, and garlic and cook until the leeks are soft, 5–7 minutes. Add the vermouth and bring to a boil. Add the thyme, parsley, and mussels and season with salt and pepper. Give the mussels a good stir, then cover the pot and steam, shaking the pot occasionally to move the mussels around. Cook until the mussels open and are cooked through, about 5 minutes. Serve the mussels hot, right from the pot, with plenty of crusty bread for dipping.

SAFFRON MUSSELS

Serves 6

4 pounds mussels

3 tablespoons olive oil

1 leek, rinsed and thinly sliced

4 cloves garlic, chopped

1 cup vermouth

½ cup cream

2 sprigs fresh thyme

2 sprigs fresh parsley, chopped

2 generous pinches saffron

Several pinches crushed red pepper

Salt

Freshly ground black pepper

THIS CREAMY SAFFRON SAUCE turns mussels into a fragrant, silky stew. I like to serve it in wide soup bowls over rice or pasta, where the mussels' black shells set off the pale yellow sauce.

1. Rinse and scrub the mussels under cold running water and debeard them by pulling off their hanging threads. Discard any cracked mussels.

2. Heat the oil in a large, heavy-bottomed pot over medium-high heat. Add the leeks and garlic and cook until the leeks are soft, 4–6 minutes. Add the vermouth, cream, thyme, parsley, and saffron and bring to a boil. Add the mussels and season with red pepper, salt, and black pepper. Give the pot a hearty stir. Cover and steam, shaking the pot occasionally to move the mussels around, until the mussels have opened, about 5 minutes. Serve hot.

194

CLAMS & SEA SNAILS MARINIÈRE

Serves 6

3 pounds small clams

3 tablespoons olive oil

1 leek, washed and thinly sliced

4 cloves garlic, chopped

2 cups dry white wine

2 sprigs fresh thyme

2 sprigs fresh parsley, chopped

1 bay leaf

Salt

Freshly ground black pepper

2 pounds sea snails

CLAMS, MORE THAN ANY OTHER MOLLUSK, become rather tough as they cook, so I make sure to use tongs to remove each hot shell to a waiting platter as soon as it opens. In France, we eat the local clams, or *palourdes,* but, realistically, at home I cook whatever clams I can find: small Littlenecks, cockles, or Manila clams. Most sea snails that we get are already cleaned and poached, so we only need to gently reheat them. Snails are a nice addition if you can find them, but it's well worth making this dish with just the clams.

1. Scrub the clam shells well to remove the sand. Heat the oil in a large, heavy-bottomed pot over medium-high heat. Add the leeks and garlic and cook until the leeks are soft, about 5 minutes. Deglaze the pot with the wine and bring to a boil. Add the thyme, parsley, and bay leaf. Season with salt and pepper.

2. Add the clams and snails, cover, and steam until the clams open and the snails are heated through, 4–6 minutes. Shake the pot occasionally to move the shells around and use tongs to remove clams from the pot as soon as they open. Serve hot with a loaf of crusty bread.

MOULES PROVENÇAL

Serves 6

4 pounds mussels

¼ cup olive oil

1 bunch green onions, white and green parts, sliced

A frond or two of fennel, chopped

4 cloves garlic, chopped

2 medium ripe tomatoes, chopped, or 1 cup canned crushed tomatoes

Pinch crushed red pepper flakes

1 cup vermouth

2 sprigs fresh thyme

2 sprigs fresh parsley, chopped

Salt

Freshly ground black pepper

Leaves from 4 sprigs fresh basil, sliced

Crusty bread, for serving

I FAVOR VERMOUTH WHEN COOKING MUSSELS, but dry white wine works perfectly. My love of vermouth comes from my chefs, especially Chris; it's just what he used! I always add just one more Provençal flavor at the very end, and it's usually basil. Or fennel. Or a dash or two of dried tarragon to deliver the hint of anise that melds perfectly with the mussels and their fragrant broth.

1. Rinse and scrub the mussels under cold running water and debeard them by pulling off their hanging threads. Discard any cracked mussels.

2. Heat the oil in a large, heavy-bottomed pot over medium-high heat. Add the green onions, fennel, and garlic and cook about 5 minutes. Add the tomatoes and red pepper flakes and deglaze the pot with the vermouth. Add the thyme, parsley, and mussels. Season with salt and pepper. Give the mussels a good stir, then cover and steam, shaking the pot occasionally to move the mussels around. Cook until the mussels open about 5 minutes. Sprinkle with the basil and serve hot with plenty of crispy bread.

MUSSEL & SWISS CHARD SOUP

Serves 6

3 pounds mussels

1 tablespoon olive oil

1 leek, washed and thinly sliced

4 cloves garlic, chopped

1 cup dry white wine

2 cups Basic Chicken Stock (page 250) or water

2 sprigs fresh thyme

Salt

Freshly ground black pepper

1 bunch Swiss chard, ribs removed and leaves shredded

THE MUSSELS ARE SO DELICATE and lightly cooked in this soup that they seem to float like little dumplings among the shredded bright green Swiss chard. I like to serve the soup as the first course of a meal that features a whole fish, like Roasted Sea Bass Provençal (page 59).

1. Rinse and scrub the mussels under cold running water and debeard them by pulling off their hanging threads. Discard any cracked mussels.

2. Heat the oil in a large, heavy-bottomed pot over medium-high heat. Add the leeks and garlic and cook until soft, about 5 minutes. Deglaze the pot with the white wine and Chicken Stock and bring to a boil. Add the thyme and mussels and season with salt and pepper. Cover and steam just until they open, about 2 minutes.

3. With a slotted spoon, transfer the mussels to a bowl. Add the Swiss chard to the pot and bring the soup to a simmer. Cook, stirring occasionally, for about 5 minutes. When you're ready to serve, drop the mussels back into the pot and warm the soup.

PAELLA OF MUSSELS, SHRIMP, CLAMS & SQUID

Serves 6

1 pound mussels

1 pound clams

3 tablespoons olive oil

1 large onion, chopped

1 red bell pepper, ribs removed, chopped

1 stalk celery, chopped

3 cloves garlic, finely chopped

½ cup thinly sliced dry chorizo sausage

Pinch saffron

Pinch crushed red pepper flakes

2 cups Arborio or Bomba rice

4 cups Basic Shrimp Stock (page 49)

1 cup fresh or canned crushed tomatoes

½ pound large wild Gulf shrimp, unpeeled, with heads attached

8 ounces squid, sliced (about 1 cup)

Salt

Freshly ground black pepper

1 cup fresh green peas

2 green onions, chopped

ONE OF THE GREATEST THINGS ABOUT THE MARKETS of Provence is the variety of street vendors and their vast steaming pans of paella, always cooked fresh before your eyes. Irresistible! You can't help stopping at their stands to sample, and the locals somehow manage to continue their shopping while devouring the fragrant plates of rice, vegetables, and seafood at the same time.

1. Rinse and scrub the mussels under cold running water and debeard them by pulling off their hanging threads. Discard any cracked mussels. Scrub the clam shells well to remove sand.

2. Heat the oil in a large paella pan or a very large skillet over medium-high heat. Add the onions, peppers, celery, and garlic and cook until tender, about 7 minutes. Add the chorizo, saffron, and pepper flakes and cook until the chorizo is browned, about 4 minutes.

3. Add the rice and stir constantly to toast the grains until they turn opaque. Add the clams, Shrimp Stock, and tomatoes and bring to a boil. Reduce the heat, cover with foil, and simmer until the rice is almost tender, about 10 minutes. Add the mussels, shrimp, and squid and simmer, uncovered, until the mussels open, about 5 minutes more. Season with salt and pepper.

4. Stir in the green peas, sprinkle with the green onions, and serve right from the pan.

VIOLETS WITH SAUCE MIGNONETTE
Serves 6

1½ pounds violet
  oysters

1 small shallot,
  finely chopped

½ cup red wine
  vinegar

1 teaspoon black
  peppercorns,
  coarsely crushed

Sea salt

THE VIOLET IS A QUINTESSENTIALLY PROVENÇAL DELICACY: it is a rare soft-shell oyster from the Mediterranean near Marseille and takes its name from the color it turns when the oyster is opened and exposed to the air. I especially like the way the writer Clifford Wright (on *ZesterDaily.com*) describes it: "The violet (*Microcosmus sulcatus*) is also known as sea fig in French, sea lemon in Italian, and cow's tit in Sicilian. I think it should be translated as sea egg. It's a mighty strange creature with a leathery skin that attaches to rocks and passes seawater through one protuberance and out another. Its meat looks like scrambled eggs and it has a distinctive taste of iodine." Of course the mignonette sauce is great on simple raw oysters, too.

1. Rinse the oysters under cold running water to remove any sand. To shuck them, insert a pointed oyster knife between the shells of each oyster, wiggle and drag the knife along the side to pop open the shell. Run the knife underneath the flesh to free it from the shell.

2. For the mignonette sauce, whisk together the shallots, vinegar, peppercorns, and salt in a small serving bowl. Nestle the violets on their half shells on a platter of crushed ice with the sauce on the side.

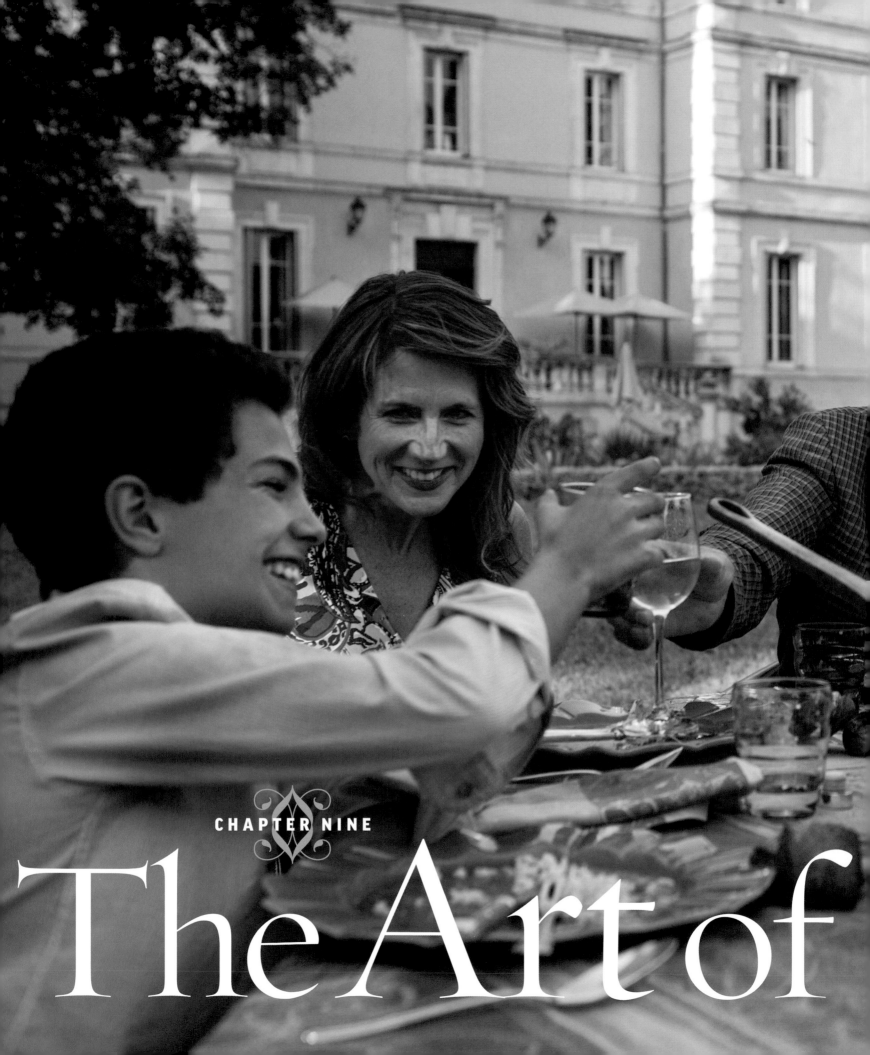

CHAPTER NINE

The Art of

the Table

L EAVING

Provence with tears in our eyes just a few years before, we never, in our wildest fantasies, could have imagined such a triumphant return. Driving in our cramped Citroën, Jenifer's maps spread across the back seat (which also held ten-day old Brendan), we never expected to come back in circumstances like these: a chance to cook *my* food in France! We were heading south across rugged land—surprised at the bounty of fruit trees and vineyards it nurtured—to the Chateau de Montcaud, in an ancient Roman outpost in a little-known département of the Gard, just across the Rhône from the famed vineyards of Châteauneuf-du-Pape. Months before, I had been introduced to a sweetheart of a man, Morris Auerbach, a good client of ours at La Provence, in

LOCAL CHÈVRES from the Alpilles, left: chestnut-wrapped Banon, soft disks dusted with pimentón and herbs, bouchons perfumed with marc de Provence. Overleaf, lunch with Armand Baur, Jenifer, Rudy and Anne Baur.

205

JENIFER AND I visit the Chateau, about 1998, above. The gated entrance, below. The open court-yard just outside the kitchen, right.

Lacombe, Louisiana, the restaurant owned by my boss and mentor, Chef Chris Kerageorgiou. Morris had agreed to help Rudy Baur, the chateau's owner, find a Louisiana chef who would spend a few weeks creating a Sunday Jazz Brunch that would be exotic enough for his French clientele, yet familiar enough for them to enjoy. Morris discussed the opportunity with my Chef Chris and with Chef Paul Prudhomme; they decided to invite *me*. What an honor to be recognized by my idols! Morris described Rudy as a Swiss-French James Bond–type, an international man of intrigue who decided to retire to the Languedoc with Anne, his beautiful young French wife. There, he renovated a centuries-old mulberry

"*When you dine with Rudy and Anne, I learned, you are never in for a quick bite. Every meal with the Baurs is an event.*"

plantation and turned it into a place where Europe's social elite could relax and enjoy the South of France, blessedly removed from the crowds and the tourists.

Rudy had built hotels around the world, but he had had enough of that corporate life and the constant travel that went with it. It was time for him to plant roots and the chateau was his dream. I was elated at the chance to cook my food for the Baurs and for weeks I'd been busily creating menus and recipes full of Provençal ideas that still reflected my Louisiana heritage.

Suddenly, seemingly out of nowhere, appeared an austere, paved wall fitted with a formidable gate, the sort of gate you'd assume a head of state lived behind. Not far from the truth, as it turned out: Rudy was a kind of sultan in his kingdom of Montcaud. Before I could reach the call button, the gate opened slowly and so we advanced, in awe of both the beauty and the refuge of the chateau's well-kept park. We arrived to a hero's welcome, Rudy and Anne with champagne glasses in hand, and a small staff to help us with our baby, the luggage, and all the seafood that I'd brought along to cook: jumbo lump blue crabmeat, crawfish tails, and sizable Louisiana white shrimp. We were whisked up to our room—an incredible dream, impeccably furnished and filled with fresh flowers. Suddenly I felt daunted. Who was I to be cooking for these folks? What in the world could I show them? Hell, they're French!

In no time we were settled in, newborn baby and all, and off to meet our hosts for dinner. Now, when you dine with Rudy and Anne, you are never in for a quick bite. A meal with the Baurs is an event. Dressed impeccably, Rudy seated us at a large circular stone banquette soft-ened by overstuffed pillows beneath a trellis of jasmine and roses, adjacent to the restaurant's dining room.

Les vins

It was in this courtyard we discussed the menu for the Jazz Brunch, sipping sparkling wine spiked with liqueurs and noshing on small Provençal bites. As Rudy explained, it's customary to begin with a crisp, light wine that's fun to drink with the salty hors d'oeuvres, in precisely the same way that we engage in small talk just after first meeting someone, one doesn't jump into deep, serious conversation until the mood mellows. Thus should the dinner progress. Seated with our new friends,

it was clear that I was in for a rare lesson in refinement. Rudy was soft-spoken and humble, yet he was so proud of the beautiful little world that he had created, he so loved sharing it. His English was perfect, his manner effortless. Originally from Switzerland and trained in the best hotel school in Lausanne, Rudy is a perfectionist on every level—always calm, cool, and gracious. His genuine smile masked his intensity as he monitored each and every guest seated in the restaurant. Once the guests retired for the evening, just about in time for our cheese course, the real Rudy emerged in boyish grins and gregarious laughter. He told stories of renovating the old house and grounds, but also about the curious ways of life of the Gard. The cheese course was always the best course with Rudy. Certainly he enjoyed everything else, but he came alive with the cheeses and loved coaching me with a great sense of ceremony through the selection of each one, from the obscure chèvre aged in marc de Provence to the supple cow's milk Saint-Marcellin, paired with the mature local reds of the Sabran, his region. But it was his spirit that touched me most: Rudy struck the perfect balance of friendliness and elegance.

My cooking debut in at the chateau eventually met with praise. Rudy and Anne asked us to return, which we did, in fact, every summer for ten years, after which I began to send my cooks there. Our children have grown in

"*I came to understand how a seemingly simple meal can be more elevated than foie gras and truffles because each element must be just perfect.*"

RUDY AND ANNE, left. Cooking with Chef René Graf and Rudy, 1996, below left. Above, the wine list, and the vineyards of the Sabran that surround the Chateau.

Learning from Rudy helped me to strip layers from my food, to focus on distinct and pure flavors, and to stop worrying about creating drama on the plate. For example, one day I prepared for him a sautéed rouget, a small red Mediterranean fish. I laid the delicate filets on an artichoke purée, then I spooned a smoky purée of beef marrow over each filet. I believed it was a masterpiece because at that time I thought of my food as most cooks do, the way I tasted it in the kitchen: one spoonful of that unctuous purée, another of that smoky marrow. Somehow it never even occurred to me to think how a guest would experience all these tastes together on one plate. Rudy told me quite directly that the marrow was one layer of flavor too many; its smokiness overwhelmed the delicacy of the rouget. He would prefer, he said, just a drop or two of good olive oil on the succulent little filets. That would have been perfect. And now it is for me, too. Lessons like that went a long way in helping me to define my style of cooking.

number, and over the years we have all shared epic tables that have been as enlightening as they've been delicious. From each meal I walk away with a more determined sense of refined hospitality that I've been blessed to try to pass on to each of my chefs. Touchingly, our return this summer marked the 16th anniversary of the Chateau de Montcaud's Sunday Jazz Brunch.

Culinary school can only offer so much; part of becoming a chef is to learn how to eat, taste, and savor. I came from a true food culture, went to the best culinary school, and had worked for some of the best chefs. But it was Rudy Baur who taught me how to *dine*. And to become a better cook in the process. I have been lucky; I've always eaten well. Very well. But when it came to haute cuisine, nobody had ever taken the time, as Rudy did, to taste, and drink, and talk with me. He taught me, by example, to think of food as the starring role in a play that needed many supporting characters to carry it from great to sublime. I had come up as a chef at a time when more was *more!* More fat, more flavor, more seasonings, and more food on the plate.

What I want our cooks to learn is what Rudy instilled in me decades ago: when you taste something you cook, imagine sitting at a table and eating the entire dish—having the entire experience. Remember, back then, fine dining still meant foie gras and truffles. I came to understand that a seemingly simple meal can be more elevated because each element must be perfect. These lessons in refinement changed the way I thought about restaurant food. In fact, they enabled me to open Restaurant August in 2001, with a clarity of vision that was worlds away from the explosive experiences happening on the plates of New Orleans restaurants at the time.

209

MY LUNCH FOR THE BAURS
It Was a Joy to Cook for These People Who Had Taught Me So Much

WHEN I RETURNED to visit the Baurs last summer, I wanted to do something special to celebrate our friendship. I wanted cook for them, but in a style that's taken me 20 years to develop; a style inspired in part by Rudy. I wanted to give the Baurs a taste of *my* Provence, influenced by my New Orleans; to express what makes Provence so special for me—those passionate ingredients and flavors so full of the sun. We began at midday, with drinks in the courtyard, creating our own apéritifs along with small bites of crisp pastry and a variety of toppings and sausages. At table for our light first course, I served a chilled fennel soup with fresh crab and heirloom tomatoes, bursting and ripe, topped with a light basil purée. The oysters I spied at Les Halles in the Avignon market that morning were too good to pass up, so on the spot I created a recipe—Oysters Gratiné with Pastis—that recalled my first visits to that market with the chateau's then-chef, René Graf, when we would stop and share a pastis with the very fishmongers who occupy that space today. Farther along the market, I was thrilled by the vivid pumpkins and squash, the abundance of wild mushrooms like chanterelles and girolles, and the big, fresh shrimp everywhere: these ingredients would come together in a perfect risotto, made with *riz de Camargue* from the coast.

For the main course, I wanted something I could carve tableside, all the better to share the bounty with my guests (who were also my hosts). I decided to make a saddle of lamb wrapped in the same herbs that those lambs grazed upon, and baked it in a beautiful salt pastry crust that infused the lamb with rosemary, thyme, and savory. I served my friends Provence on a plate: the herb-scented lamb, a creamy porridge of *panisse* made from chickpeas, a luscious eggplant and

tomato confit bathed in fine local olive oil, crispy fried squash blossoms, and succulent caramelized figs.

Cheese is Rudy's soft spot, so I was happy to find beautiful Banon, a Provençal chèvre wrapped in its signature chestnut leaf and tied with raffia, and some tiny crottins. I met a woman at the market who made her chèvres from the milk of goats that graze wild in the nearby Alpilles. She rolled some of her cheeses in spices like pimentón, some in herb leaves and olives, and cured others in marc. I loaded a platter with grapes so fresh they looked like they'd jumped the fence from the surrounding vineyards. I sliced a couple of the famed melons of Cavaillon, filled bowls with perfect peaches, and figs, both fresh and dried, and I drizzled giant nutmeats of walnut and almond with my favorite lavender honey. For dessert, I decided on a warm apricot tart, not very different from those I cooked on my very first trip to Provence so long ago, but this time I finished it with a spicy touch of cardamom, and served it with lavender honey ice cream. Our feast culminated in a guitar serenade by Armand Baur, age 11. What did he play? "When the Saints Come Marching In"! *Bien sûr.*

PERFECT HORS D'OEUVRES, from left: Black Olive Tapenade, Black Olive Fougasse, Green Almond Paste, Green Olive Tapenade, Anchoïade.

THE APÉRITIF TRADITION

I AM SO FOND of the French idea of the apéritif—not just for the sake of nostalgia, but because this playful occasion has a real purpose: to lighten us up. The apéritif is not just a bridge to a meal; it's a social event in itself. Throughout the region, from Haute-Provence to the watery Bouches-du-Rhône, there is a tradition of making liqueurs and fortifying wines with mountain herbs, or dark walnuts, or oranges, or peaches or sour cherries. Sharing a sip with a neighbor or friend is a small celebration in itself.

I love the way any *vin de pays* can be elevated with just a drop of cassis. Kir and Kir Royale (with Champagne) are so delicious they became a cliché, along with other apéritif standards Dubonnet, Lillet, and Pineau des Charentes. Today you'd probably be laughed out of your trendy bar if you ordered one. We're living in the age of the dead serious bartender who all but worships what he drinks. Our bartenders go to such great lengths to make their own bitters, but are they any better than Peychaud's or Angostura? We've become so serious about drink, we forget to have fun. Which is why I love the hour of the apéritif. I like to have a few bottles of white wine and Champagne open along with several flavored liqueurs and let people create their own drinks. It lightens up the conversation and loosens the mood. Apéritifs are especially good while nibbling deliciously crispy cheese straws and smoothly salty spreads.

BLACK OLIVE FOUGASSE

Makes 1 loaf

¾ cup warm water

1 tablespoon sugar

1 packet (.75 ounce) yeast

4 cups bread flour, plus more for kneading

1 tablespoon salt

Olive oil

¼ cup chopped olives

Handful whole olives (optional)

FOUGASSE IS THE PROVENÇAL VERSION OF FOCACCIA, the Italian flatbread, and there are as many ways to shape it as there are cooks. Often in Provence you'll find *grattons,* crisped pork skins, folded into the batter instead of black olives. I like to cut the baked *fougasse* into long breadsticks to enjoy with hors d'oeuvre spreads like Goat Cheese Mousse (page 216), Black or Green Olive Tapenade, and Green Almond Paste. This recipe has chopped olives mixed into the dough, but I also love *fougasse* with whole olives pressed into the flattened dough just before it goes into the oven. My Chef Chris would instruct us to punch the dough down with our fingertips, leaving dimples in the dough. You'd pour on enough olive oil to fill the dimples and, sometimes, slip olives into them.

1. Put ¼ cup of the warm water in a small bowl and stir in the sugar. Sprinkle the yeast on top and let it stand until foamy, about 5 minutes.

2. Combine the flour and salt in the bowl of a stand mixer fitted with a dough hook. With the mixer on, add the yeast mixture, remaining ½ cup warm water, 2 tablespoons olive oil, and the chopped olives. Knead in the mixer bowl until a soft, sticky dough forms, about 5 minutes. Turn the dough out onto a well-floured surface and knead another 5 minutes, adding more flour if the dough seems too sticky. Put the dough into a large, well-oiled bowl, cover with plastic wrap, and set in a warm place in your kitchen. Let the dough rise until it has doubled in size, about 1 hour.

3. Preheat the oven to 375°. Punch down the dough and transfer to an oiled baking pan. Cover with plastic wrap and let rest another 30 minutes. Uncover, dimple the dough, and coat with olive oil, poking whole olives into the dimples if you like. Bake until golden brown, about 30 minutes.

ANCHOÏADE

Makes about 1 cup

20 filets salt-cured anchovies

1 cup olive oil

3 cloves garlic, crushed

½ cup crumbled day-old country bread

1 tablespoon vinegar

Freshly ground black pepper

THIS ANCHOVY PASTE uses dry bread to help emulsify the ingredients and make it more substantial and less oily than most *anchoïades*. Chef Chris used to add blanched green almonds to his anchovy paste, but since they are really difficult to find, day-old bread does the texture trick. Salt-cured or good oil-cured anchovies make all the difference in flavor and character.

1. Rinse the anchovies under cold water for a minute or so. Put them in a skillet with 2 tablespoons of the olive oil and the garlic and mash them with the back of a fork over high heat. This heating and mashing wakes the anchovies up and softens the garlic a bit so it doesn't overpower the anchovies.

2. Once the garlic has softened, transfer the mixture to the bowl of a food processor and add the bread and vinegar. Blend while slowly adding the rest of the olive oil. Season with pepper.

GREEN ALMOND PASTE

Makes about 1 ½ cups

1 cup fresh green
almonds, peeled

2 cloves garlic

1 filet salt-cured
anchovy, rinsed

1 tablespoon capers

1 tablespoon sherry
vinegar

½ cup olive oil

Salt

Freshly ground
black pepper

GREEN ALMONDS ARE MOST OFTEN FOUND in markets in late spring and throughout the summer. They have a sweet, delicate flavor and are used throughout Provençal cooking as a thickener for purées and soups. When I can get my hands on some, I make this lovely dip for crisp bread or raw vegetables.

1. Bring a small saucepan of water to a boil. Add the almonds and garlic and blanch for about 30 seconds. Drain and rinse under cold water. Transfer the almonds and garlic to the bowl of a food processor and add the anchovy, capers, and vinegar. Blend while slowly pouring in the olive oil. Season with salt and pepper.

BLACK OR GREEN OLIVE TAPENADE

Makes about 2 cups

2 cups pitted olives

2 cloves garlic,
peeled

2 filets salt-cured
anchovies

1 tablespoon capers

Leaves from
1 sprig fresh
thyme

½ cup olive oil

THERE ARE MANY STYLES AND COLORS of tapenade spread, depending, of course, on the olives you use. I love picholine, Lucques, and even the tiny black olives of Nice, but most often I use oil-cured black olives and, always, the defining capers.

1. Combine the olives, garlic, anchovies, capers, and thyme in the bowl of a food processor and pulse until the olives are coarsely chopped. With the machine running, slowly add the olive oil until it is all absorbed.

215

PAILLETTES: QUICK PUFF PASTRY HORS D'OEUVRES

Serves 8–10

1 sheet puff pastry dough, defrosted

1 egg

2 tablespoons milk

½ cup finely grated Parmesan cheese

2-3 pinches cayenne pepper

IMPROMPTU hors d'oeuvres depend on good-quality frozen puff pastry dough; always keep some in your freezer. It's so easy to turn a sheet of pastry into cheese straws, in many shapes and flavors. Slice, bake, and *voila!* A salty crusty nibble with your fruity Kir.

1. Preheat the oven to 375°. Lay the pastry on a lightly floured surface. Lightly beat the egg with the milk and, with a pastry brush, coat the dough with the egg mixture. Dust with the Parmesan and cayenne. Roll the dough into a jelly roll cylinder and slice into pinwheels about ¼ inch thick. Lay them on a baking pan and bake until golden brown, 15–20 minutes.

Variation: Spread about ½ cup Black or Green Olive Tapenade (page 215) on the puff pastry instead of Parmesan, and roll into palmiers, as pictured.

FRESH HERBED GOAT CHEESE MOUSSE

Makes about 1 cup

1 cup (about 8 ounces) fresh goat cheese

⅓ cup cream

½ small bunch fresh chives, chopped

Handful chopped fresh herbs

Pinch salt

Freshly ground black pepper

ANY FRESH GOAT CHEESE will work well here: I love the Provençal Brousse, whose special flavor comes from the wild herbs the goats graze on, but any soft goat cheese, or even good ricotta, will make a tasty dip. I like to serve it with salty Paillettes, above, and Fougasse (page 214), but it's just as good (and faster) on small toasts.

1. Soften the cheese with the cream in a small bowl and whisk in the chives and herbs. Season with salt and pepper.

OYSTERS GRATINÉ WITH PASTIS

Serves 4

12 oysters

1 tablespoon olive oil

1 small shallot, finely chopped

1 clove garlic, finely chopped

1 sprig fresh thyme

¼ cup dry white wine

¼ cup liquor from the oysters, or Basic Shrimp Stock (page 49)

¼ cup heavy cream

2 tablespoons pastis

2 egg yolks

1 tablespoon lemon juice

Dash Tabasco

Pinch saffron

Salt

Freshly ground black pepper

THE DELICIOUS PASTIS CREAM can be made in advance so all you have to do is top the oysters in their half shells just before you're ready to broil and serve them.

1. Preheat the broiler. Shuck the oysters and keep them on the half shell. Reserve their liquor. Place the oysters on a baking pan. Heat the olive oil in a small saucepan over high heat. Add the shallot, garlic, and thyme and cook for a minute, then add the wine, oyster liquor or Shrimp Stock, cream, and pastis and bring to a boil.

2. In a separate bowl, beat the egg yolks, then slowly ladle in about ½ cup of the hot stock while still beating the yolks. Pour the egg mixture back into the saucepan, then add the lemon juice, Tabasco, and saffron and stir, whisking, for a couple of minutes, until the liquid has thickened enough to coat the back of a spoon. Season with salt and pepper.

3. Spoon the sauce over each oyster. Slip the pan under the broiler and broil until the oysters are browned, about 3 minutes, then serve.

FENNEL SOUP WITH CRAB & PISTOU

Serves 6

3 tablespoons olive oil

1 leek, chopped

2 cloves garlic, sliced

1 large fennel bulb, chopped

1 large yellow potato, peeled and chopped

1 bay leaf

5 cups Basic Chicken Stock (page 250)

½ cup cream

Salt

Freshly ground black pepper

1 medium tomato, peeled and diced

2 teaspoons sherry vinegar

4 ounces lump jumbo blue crabmeat

Fresh basil sprigs

FOR THE PISTOU

Handful fresh basil leaves

¼ cup olive oil

3 cloves garlic, peeled

Pinch grated Parmesan cheese

THIS LIGHT, CREAMY FENNEL SOUP is related to my Basic Vichyssoise (page 246). I serve the soup cold over a little crabmeat salad made with the Mediterranean spider crab readily found in Provence. At home I use lump blue crabmeat instead.

1. Heat 2 tablespoons of the olive oil in a medium pot over medium-high heat. Add the leeks, garlic, fennel, and potatoes and cook until the leeks and fennel are softened, about 5 minutes. Add the bay leaf, Chicken Stock, and cream and simmer until the potatoes are very tender, about 25 minutes. Discard the bay leaf. Transfer the soup to a blender and blend until very smooth. Season with salt and pepper. Refrigerate until ready to serve.

2. Toss the tomatoes in a medium bowl with the sherry vinegar and the remaining 1 tablespoon olive oil. Season with salt and pepper.

3. To make the Pistou, purée the basil, olive oil, and garlic in a blender, then stir in the Parmesan.

4. Divide the tomatoes, crab, and basil sprigs among 6 soup bowls and ladle in the soup. Drizzle each bowl with the Pistou.

219

SHRIMP, CHANTERELLE & PUMPKIN RISOTTO

Serves 6

3 tablespoons olive oil

½ onion, chopped

2 cups Arborio rice

1 sprig fresh rosemary

5-6 cups Basic Chicken Stock (page 250)

2 cups diced peeled fresh pumpkin

1 pound large wild Gulf shrimp, peeled and deveined

Salt

Freshly ground black pepper

1½ cups chanterelles or other wild mushrooms

½ cup grated Parmesan cheese

4 tablespoons butter, cut into small chunks

½ small bunch fresh chives, chopped

Leaves from 2 sprigs fresh thyme

CERTAINLY ANY WILD MUSHROOM will work in this risotto, and any hearty fall squash can replace the pumpkin. In Southern France, I like to use *riz de Camargue,* a round white rice which is like the Spanish Bomba rice. Both cook in the same way as Arborio, making a creamy, luscious risotto.

1. Heat the oil in a large, heavy-bottomed pot over high heat. Add the onions and cook, stirring with a wooden spoon, until soft, about 5 minutes. Add the rice and stir for another minute. Add the rosemary sprig, cover with 2 cups Chicken Stock, and bring to a boil. Reduce the heat to medium low, cover the pot, and simmer for about 5 minutes. Add another cup or two of Chicken Stock and the pumpkin. Stir well, then cover and simmer for 10 minutes.

2. Season the shrimp with salt and pepper and add to the pot along with the mushrooms and the remaining Chicken Stock. Raise the heat to medium and cook about 5 minutes, stirring occasionally. Test the rice for doneness: It should be soft, with a slight bite in the center. Remove the sprig of rosemary and fold in the Parmesan, butter, and chives. Season with salt and pepper and scatter thyme leaves on top. Serve immediately.

AT THE CHATEAU with 10-day old Brendan, 1996, left. Preparing my first Jazz Brunch on the grounds, in 1996, above.

SADDLE OF LAMB WRAPPED IN SALT PASTRY

Serves 6

3 egg whites

Couple handfuls fresh herbs such as thyme, marjoram, sage, or savory

1 cup kosher salt

2 cups flour

Freshly ground black pepper

6 branches fresh rosemary

2 pounds boneless lamb loin roast

1 pint black mission figs, halved

1 teaspoon sugar

BAKING MEAT WRAPPED in a salt pastry is an old, time-tested technique. We're really steaming the loin of lamb and infusing it with the flavor of the herbs that grow wild in the hills all over Provence. Since we're not eating the pastry, don't worry about the amount of salt used in the crust. I love the ceremony of breaking into the crust in front of my guests, with the fragrant herby steam escaping. It's quite a show.

1. Preheat the oven to 425°. For the dough, whisk the egg whites in a large bowl until frothy. Add the herbs, salt, and ½ cup cold water. Stir in the flour and knead until the dough pulls away from the sides of the bowl.

2. Roll the dough out on a well-floured surface until it is about ¼ inch thick. Season with salt and pepper and lay the rosemary branches over the dough. Fold the dough around the lamb and pinch the seams together. Trim off the excess pastry. Place on a baking pan and bake until golden brown, about 15 minutes. Remove to a cutting board.

3. Meanwhile, heat a large skillet over medium-high heat. Sprinkle the figs with the sugar. Put the figs, cut-side down, in the skillet and sear until caramelized, about 2 minutes.

4. To serve the lamb, bring the cutting board to the table, cut through the pastry, and slice the lamb, discarding the pastry and rosemary. Serve with the caramelized figs, along with the Creamy Panisse, Eggplant & Tomato Confit, and Fried Squash Blossoms (page 225).

EGGPLANT & TOMATO CONFIT

Serves 6

1 medium eggplant, peeled and diced

1 sprig fresh thyme

1 cup olive oil

2 cloves garlic, thinly sliced

2 pints cherry tomatoes, peeled

Sherry vinegar

Salt

Freshly ground black pepper

Leaves from 2 sprigs fresh basil

I CALL THIS *CONFIT* because slow-cooking the eggplant in the oven gives it such a soft and luscious consistency; it absorbs the olive oil in a way that's reminiscent of preserved eggplant. I'll often make the eggplant in advance, then finish it with the tomatoes.

1. Preheat the oven to 400°. In a small saucepan, combine the eggplant, thyme, and olive oil. Cover the pan with foil and bake 30 minutes, until the eggplant has absorbed the oil.

2. Meanwhile, in a medium skillet over medium-high heat, sweat the garlic in a tablespoon of olive oil. Add the cherry tomatoes and a dash of sherry vinegar and cook to soften the tomatoes, about 5 minutes.

3. Add the eggplant confit to the tomatoes, season with salt and pepper, sprinkle with the basil, and serve.

224

CREAMY PANISSE

Serves 6

3 cups Basic Chicken Stock (page 250)

2 cloves garlic, finely chopped

1 cup chickpea flour

3 tablespoons olive oil

½ cup grated Parmesan cheese

Leaves from 1 sprig fresh thyme

1 teaspoon lemon zest

1 teaspoon salt

Pinch cayenne pepper

THINK OF *PANISSE* as polenta or grits made from chickpea flour instead of corn. On the Mediterranean coast around Nice, *panisse* is fried into crispy chickpea French fries. But here I make it creamy, the way I would polenta, and think it's delicious with grated cheese served with Saddle of Lamb Wrapped in Salt Pastry (page 222).

1. Bring the Chicken Stock and garlic to a boil in a large saucepan. While the stock is boiling, whisk in the chickpea flour. Once the pan returns to a boil, reduce the heat to medium low and simmer, stirring occasionally, for 15 minutes. Stir in the olive oil, Parmesan, thyme, lemon zest, salt, and cayenne. Spoon onto a serving plate and serve.

FRIED SQUASH BLOSSOMS

Serves 6

Canola oil

1 cup flour

1 egg

12 squash blossoms

Salt

SIMILAR TO OUR Stuffed Zucchini Blossoms (page 154), this crispy fried version adds a welcome texture and a lovely floral flavor to the luscious lamb (page 222), while still staying true to the vegetable palette of Provence.

1. Heat about 3 inches oil in a medium, heavy-bottomed pot over medium heat until it reaches 350° on a candy thermometer. In a large bowl, whisk together the flour, egg, and 1 cup ice water. Dip the squash blossoms, a few at a time, into the batter. In batches, gently drop them into the hot oil and fry until golden brown, 1–2 minutes. As they are done, drain them on paper towels and sprinkle with salt. Serve immediately.

LAVENDER HONEY ICE CREAM WITH PISTACHIOS

Serves 6 (Makes about 5 cups)

1½ cups heavy cream

1½ cups whole milk

½ cup sugar

4 egg yolks

¼ cup lavender honey

½ teaspoon salt

Toasted pistachios, chopped

I FELL IN LOVE WITH LAVENDER HONEY the first time I went to Provence. Its subtle floral undertones had such great flavor and this ice cream became my very favorite. You can use any honey you love instead of the lavender honey. But I wouldn't! I like to serve it with a warm tart, but it is perfect on its own.

1. Heat the cream and milk with ¼ cup of the sugar in a small saucepan over medium heat until simmering. Meanwhile, whisk the yolks with the remaining ¼ cup sugar in a bowl until pale yellow and thickened. Add about a quarter of the hot milk to the yolk mixture, a tablespoon at a time and whisking vigorously, to temper the yolks.

2. Turn the heat to low and whisk the milk and yolk mixture back into the pan. Cook until the mixture is thickened enough to coat the back of a spoon, 2–3 minutes. Stir in the lavender honey and salt.

3. Freeze in an ice cream maker following the manufacturer's directions.

WARM APRICOT TART

Serves 6

FOR THE STREUSEL

1 cup shelled pistachios, toasted

¼ cup packed light brown sugar

2 tablespoons cold butter

2 tablespoons flour

2 teaspoons grated orange zest

Pinch ground cardamom

½ teaspoon salt

FOR THE TART

Basic Sweet Tart Dough (page 278)

8 apricots, pitted and sliced

3 tablespoons honey

1 tablespoon flour

ANY STONE FRUIT WILL WORK incredibly well in this recipe, so feel free to use peaches, plums, nectarines, or a combination of all those delicious fruits. I like to serve the tart with my favorite Lavender Honey Ice Cream, above.

1. Preheat the oven to 350°. For the streusel topping, combine the pistachios, brown sugar, butter, flour, zest, cardamom, and salt in the bowl of a food processor. Pulse until the pistachios are coarsely chopped and the butter and flour form pea-sized lumps.

2. For the tart, roll out the dough and line a tart pan or pie dish. In a large bowl, toss the apricots with the honey and flour and pour into the prepared pie pan. Bake 20 minutes. Top with the streusel, return to the oven, and bake about 25 minutes, until the topping is golden.

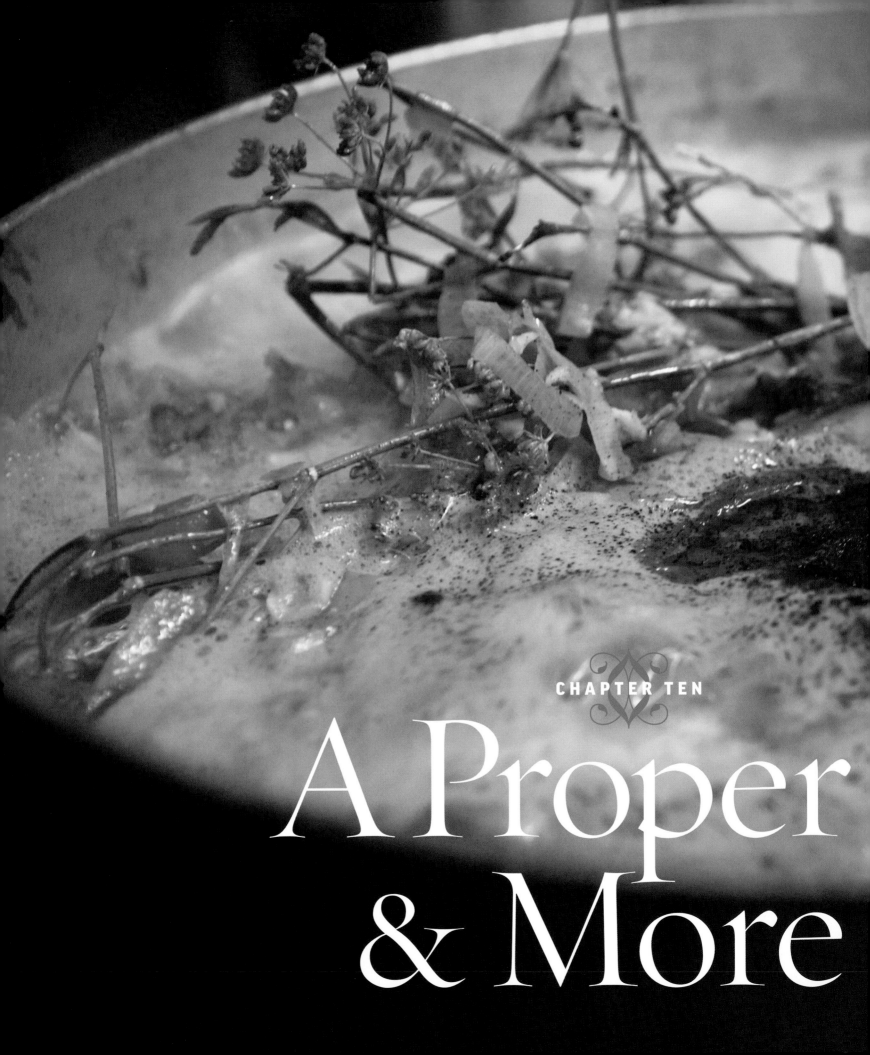

A Proper
& More

Bouillabaisse
Soup Lessons

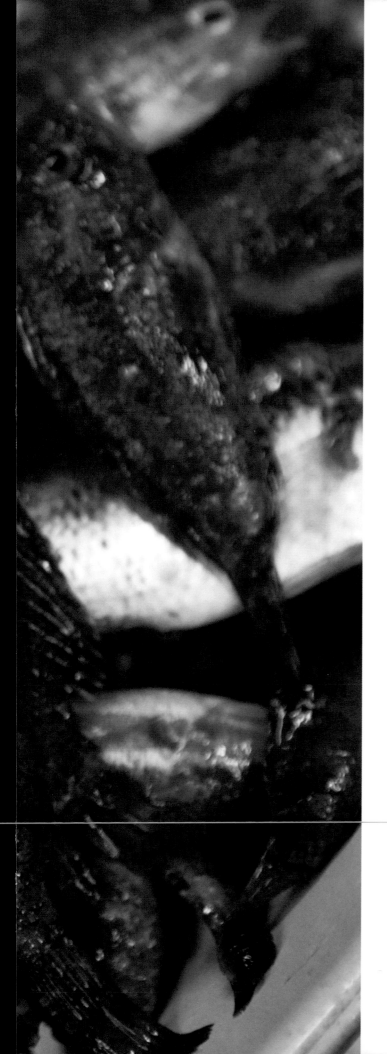

T

HOUGH HE HAS no reindeer, beard, belly, or North Pole, I always think of Alain Assaud as a jolly, caring Santa Claus in his kitchen workshop of the Bouches-du-Rhône, where he even performs magic tricks (besides the cooking) and his apprentice's elfin charm is contagious. Looking at Chef Alain, you behold bright, happy, dancing black eyes above rosy cheeks that bracket a heartfelt smile. He has a few grey hairs (as I do); they tell a story of the masterful artistry of his craft. His hands are butcher strong, yet as restrained as a sculptor's. He orchestrates his pots and pans, knives and flames with the ease of a seasoned composer. Yet his demeanor is humble, if not meek, which makes him that much more enjoyable to be around. As does the knowledge that he comes

TINY ROCKFISH, left, found only along the Mediterranean coast, add their distinctive flavor to Alain Assaud's Soupe de Poissons. Overleaf, when the saffron hits the pot of soup, you know dinner's just an hour away.

231

to his restaurant with a better résumé than most of the world's three-star chefs. His CV is studded with years of serious work under some of the best modern French chefs in history, including Alain Chapel, Roger Vergé, Michel Guérard, plus stints at l'Oustau de Baumanière and les Frères Troisgros, to name a few.

Many of my fellow chefs (with only half Alain's experience and expertise) have become famous jet-setters, dashing between restaurants in New York, London, Hong Kong, and Paris. But not Alain Assaud. He is at peace and at home in St.-Rémy-de-Provence, where he looks after elderly neighbors and raises his eight-year-old daughter. Chef Alain has chosen to stand behind his well-worn stoves, among stacks of ancient steamer pots, heavy *sautoirs,* and earthenware *daubières,* in his small, very personal restaurant and produce some of the most

delicious cooking in Provence. I met Chef Alain almost by accident, while rambling through the delectable streets of St.-Rémy one market day many summers ago while I was cooking at the Chateau de Montcaud for Chef René Graf. I had heard about this man who'd left the three-starred Michelin world to focus on the simple, peasant-based foods of his childhood; I was awestruck when I stumbled upon him prepping for the evening in an irresistibly small and quaint restaurant. At that time (1995), this was unheard of: No chef in his right mind would give up stars to cook from the heart. That was borderline insanity! That was Alain Assaud!

Over the intervening dozen or so years, I would make my pilgrimage to Alain's restaurant to pay homage, not just to the man who became my friend, but to a style of cooking that was in grave danger of becoming extinct, kidnapped as it was by the shameful tourist haunts that I fear will spell the demise of the noble Provençal peasant cuisine. Alain saw this erosion coming long ago. His choices inspired me to realize that a similar dilution of a

MY FRIEND THE CHEF: with Alain Assaud at his restaurant, far left. At the Poissonerie, above. In old St-Rémy, left.

"I wanted to pay homage not just to my friend Alain Assaud, but to a style of cooking that is in danger of becoming extinct."

cuisine didn't impress me as much as his willingness to share it with others. I believe our similar heritages—both of us born into places of strong regional cultures and cuisines—inspired me to write my first book, *My New Orleans.* Alain's work guided me to consider my own childhood dishes like gumbo and jambalaya with new respect. Though his food was worlds apart from our local flavors, it was the spirit of Alain's Provence that was utterly familiar to my New Orleans.

Throughout our friendship, Alain welcomed me into the small world of his kitchen, where he alone does the cooking. On paper ripped from his cash register, I'd jot down recipes as I peeled, chopped, and diced for him, peppering him with questions as if I were a journalist or food historian, which in a sense I was. For once, it paid to play the dumb American: I made it my mission to learn what Alain knew from his heart. With almost no written recipes, Alain cooks like a Provençal grandmother; he cooks like my Chef Chris from New Orleans, who was born in Provence—sophisticated, yet very real. A clove or two of garlic for every guest real! Like Chef Chris, he abhors short cuts; he lives for the mortar and pestle and he loves the food mill, both far more dear to him than any food processor could ever be.

My recent cooking session with Alain proved the most enjoyable, because this time I brought my colleagues: cookbook editor, photographer, documentary filmmaker, and recipe editor along with two of my cooks to observe Alain in his tiny kitchen as he made a *soupe de poissons,* a classic fish soup that's the basis of bouillabaisse. Alain wanted us to share a lunch with a few friends and I wanted to document this special experience. Every lunch he serves depends on what's in the market and especially what's at his local fishmonger's. Shopping for fish

beautiful culture was happening in my own New Orleans backyard. In the same way that home cooks no longer passed the old food traditions of Provence along to the next generation, we were in danger of losing our Creole culture and New Orleans culinary traditions. That is, if we chefs didn't do something about it. Alain has inspired me in other ways too: to truly understand the history of these time-honored foods and thus retain the soul of a recipe. The fact that this much-lauded chef cared to embrace preservationist

inevitably means a celebratory pastis at the impeccable Poissonnerie Saint-Rémoise, around the corner from Assaud's restaurant. Alain talks his way through the catch, carefully examining the pristine condition of the perfect little rockfish, or *poissons de roche,* that come from the salt marsh estuaries of the Camargue, caught along the jetties at the mouth of the Rhône where it empties into the salty Mediterranean. As far as Alain is concerned, if the little green Provençal crabs called *favouilles* aren't available, he'll be happy with these tiny rockfish.

A fine *soupe de poissons* is the living heart of the famed bouillabaisse, so, with a couple of kilos of tiny fish in hand we hurry back to his kitchen where onion, leeks, garlic, tomatoes, and celery are cut up for a great well-worn pot, then smothered with saffron and fennel stalks. Alain makes an ingenious bouquet garni from a single leek frond wrapped around herb branches and tied with string. Using white wine and water, what could be dismissed as bycatch fish are set to simmer for the better part of an hour, and gradually transformed into a russet broth. It's important to note that as long as there is something to cut and cook, the time in the kitchen is all serious professionalism. But once the *soupe de poissons* is

"Alain stops, looks into my eyes, and explains that if he were making a bouillabaisse, he'd add water to the strained fish for a second broth."

simmering away, it's time to engage in a pastis or two—another similarity of our two live-and-let-live cultures.

As the masterpiece begins to cook down to its proper consistency, the mood becomes serious again. It's time to pass the soup through a chinois, a conical funnel, with enough force to extract every ounce of luscious broth from the soft bones of the small fish. Then Alain turns his attention to the *rouille,* the traditional sauce he makes by hand, pounding garlic, egg yolks, olive oil, and saffron in a vast, ancient olivewood mortar, adding a generous amount of Moroccan harissa, which, the chef explains, was originally roasted and minced cayenne

peppers. In school we were taught rouille as a garlic mayonnaise with roasted red peppers made in a blender. Watching Alain work with mortar and pestle, it's clear that the power of this sauce comes from the power he puts into making it by hand. Rustic and potent, rouille, which takes its name from the French word for rust (which Alain charmingly illustrates by pointing to a rusty spot on his metal kitchen door), is used to both season and thicken the soup, which would not be the same without it. Rouille is always served on toasted baguette rounds with the soup ladled over, which creates an emulsion of soup and sauce.

WORKING together in Assaud's tiny kitchen, left. Well-used ladle, above. Alain's notebook, right. Getting ready for lunch in the restaurant, below.

At this point Alain stops, looks into my eyes, and explains that if he were making a bouillabaisse, which is served in two courses, he would take the remains of the strained fish from the soup and make a second broth by adding water to it and bringing it to a simmer for an hour or so. In that flavorful broth he would poach pieces of monkfish, cod, and other white saltwater fish. Alain explains that this was how poor fishermen would get several meals from whatever small fish they hadn't sold. Cook the fish once to make the *soupe de poissons,* and save what some would consider waste to create the second part of a bouillabaisse—whole fish poached in fish broth with potatoes, both served with rouille.

Although I learned nothing new that day, because Alain had many times articulated the nuances of bouillabaisse to me, and though I loved hearing it again, what moved me most was the sight of my friends in awe of Alain. It became a spiritual moment for us all—being in the presence of this great artisan whose passions transcend language barriers. Then Alain Assaud sat down with us and broke crusty bread and drank some good wine. And we were lucky enough to live, even for a moment, like a Provençal, basking in garlicky fish soup and two heaping spoonfuls of laughter.

ALAIN'S SOUPE DE POISSONS

Serves 8

FOR THE SOUP

¼ cup olive oil

12 small blue crabs, crushed

1 large onion, chopped

2 fennel bulbs, chopped, stalks reserved

1 leek, chopped

1 stalk celery, chopped

1 teaspoon fennel seeds, crushed

2 pounds fish heads, gills removed

Cloves from 1 head garlic, peeled and crushed

2 pinches saffron

½ teaspoon cayenne pepper

6 tomatoes, quartered

¼ cup tomato paste

Salt

Freshly ground black pepper

Alain's Bouquet Garni page (page 244)

24 baguette rounds

Olive oil

A few cloves garlic, peeled

Rouille (page 241)

Grated cheese such as Gruyère

MAKING SOUPE DE POISSONS is an adventure on many levels. This soup is bright with the flavors of just the right ingredients that come from wherever you're making it. The process is important, too, adding those ingredients at just the right moment. Knowing that it's pretty much impossible to find the tiny rockfish or the Mediterranean *favouille* crabs that Alain uses in his soup, it is the spirit of his soup that I replicate in this recipe. Our blue crabs mimic the flavor of *favouilles*. Sure they're different, but no less authentic in America. I find a deeper flavor results from crushing the crabs in a plastic bag with a meat mallet to catch every bit of luscious juice. In Alain's kitchen (see Cooking Lesson, page 238), he passes the finished soup through a strainer and saves the fish solids. Those he puts in a pot, covers with water, and simmers into a flavorful broth for poaching white fish filets for Bouillabaisse, or for his Grand Aïoli (page 181). Alain pours pastis, below.

1. For the soup, heat the oil in a large, heavy-bottomed pot over medium-high heat. Add the crushed crabs and stir until the shells turn red, about 10 minutes, toasting the crabs to bring out the flavor. Add the onions, chopped fennel, leeks, celery, and fennel seeds and cook for about 3 minutes. Stir in the fish heads, garlic, saffron, and cayenne and cook, stirring, for another 5 minutes. Add the tomatoes and tomato paste and cook, stirring, until the tomatoes are softened, about 10 minutes. Add water to cover the fish by 1 inch. Season with salt and pepper.

2. Once the soup comes to a boil, add the fennel stalks and the Bouquet Garni. Reduce the heat to medium low and simmer, skimming off the foam as it rises to the surface, until the soup is rich with the flavors of the fish and vegetables, about 1 hour. Strain the soup through a fine mesh strainer or chinois into another pot. (Consider retaining the solids to make another poaching liquid.)

3. To serve, brush the bread with olive oil and toast on both sides. Rub the toasts with the peeled garlic, top with generous dollops of Rouille, and place in the bottom of soup bowls. Ladle the hot soup over the toasts, sprinkle with the cheese, and serve.

1. In Alain's kitchen, he uses tiny fresh Mediterranean rockfish straight from the Poissonerie St-Rémoise.

2. Heat the oil in a large, heavy-bottomed pot and cook the onions, fennel bulb, leeks, and celery until tender.

5. Add quartered, ripe tomatoes to the pot and cook until the tomatoes melt into the broth.

6. Alain uses fresh fennel stalks and flowers from the garden to enhance the seasoning of the broth.

3. Peel lots of fresh garlic. Add half to the pot and save the rest for the Rouille (page 241).

4. Add all of the whole tiny rockfish to the pot and stir well to mix with the vegetables.

7. Add the fennel stalks and Bouquet Garni (page 244), and simmer the soup until rich and flavorful, about 1 hour.

8. Strain the soup through a chinois, making sure to crush the tiny fish with a large wooden spoon.

1. Finely chop fresh garlic cloves and add a pinch of salt to help crush the garlic. Transfer to a mortar or bowl.

2. Add the saffron powder and use the pestle to crush the chopped garlic into a smooth paste.

3. Whisk in the yolks and lemon juice and then add the olive oil slowly, whisking as you go.

4. Make the signature rusty color of Rouille by whisking the harissa into the olive oil and garlic mixture.

ROUILLE

Serves 8

6 cloves garlic, finely
  chopped

Salt

3 generous pinches
  saffron powder

2 egg yolks

Juice of ½ lemon

2 cups olive oil

2 tablespoons
  harissa

THIS INTENSE, CREAMY peppery sauce is traditional with Bouillabaisse and all fish soups. Alain makes his by hand in an ancient olivewood mortar and pestle. Not everyone is lucky enough to have those; a whisk and bowl will work well, just make sure the garlic is finely chopped before you begin. The Moroccan harissa Alain prefers lends its signature rusty color. It can be very spicy, so use as much as you like. (You can substitute chile paste.) I like my Rouille to be so hot my head sweats.

1. Crush the garlic with a healthy pinch of salt in a large mortar or bowl until you have a smooth garlic paste. Add the saffron and continue to pound.

2. Now use a whisk to whip together the luscious paste, adding the yolks and lemon juice. Whisking vigorously, slowly add the olive oil. Once the mixture comes together, add the harissa. Season with more salt.

5. To serve the soup, rub a toasted baguette slice with garlic and top with a generous dollop of Rouille.

CHRIS'S BOUILLABAISSE

Serves 8

½ pound monkfish, cut in pieces

2 6–8-ounce filets red snapper, skin on, scaled, cut in pieces

4 whole porgies or croakers, gutted and scaled

1 pound cod or hake filet, cut in pieces

4 tablespoons olive oil

6 cloves garlic, peeled and crushed

1 teaspoon cayenne pepper

2 pinches saffron

1 branch fresh thyme

Salt

Freshly ground black pepper

1 leek, chopped

1 fennel frond, chopped

3 tomatoes, chopped

Soupe de Poissons (page 237)

6-8 medium potatoes, peeled and quartered

Rouille (page 241)

THIS VERSION OF BOUILLABAISSE honors the spirit of the classic, which is far more important than hunting down versions of Mediterranean fish that are a) impossible to find, and b) inappropriate because that misses the point of the local freshness of this iconic fish stew. My mentor Chris Kerageorgiou was born in Port-Saint-Louis, just outside Marseille. Of course the fish he found in his adopted New Orleans was very different from the Mediterranean varieties he grew up with. But the Bouillabaisse I learned from him was no less delicious for the necessary substitutions. Here, we're gently poaching the fish (which has been briefly marinated) in the aromatic and intensely flavorful Soupe de Poissons. Bouillabaisse is usually served in two courses; first the soup, then the poached fish. It's important to remove the fish from the soup to a serving platter the instant it's cooked.

1. On a large platter, combine the monkfish, snapper, porgy, and cod with 2 tablespoons of the olive oil, the garlic, cayenne pepper, saffron, thyme, salt, and pepper. Marinate for 30 minutes.

2. In a large heavy-bottomed pot, heat the remaining 2 tablespoons olive oil. Add the leeks, fennel, and tomatoes and sauté until soft. Add the Soupe de Poissons and the potatoes and bring to a boil. Simmer for 20 minutes or until the potatoes are almost cooked.

3. With the soup at a bare simmer, add the marinated fish, first the whole porgy, then the pieces, and gently poach until they become translucent, 7–10 minutes. Remove the poached fish and the potatoes to a platter with a slotted spoon. Strain the soup and serve in soup bowls with dollops of Rouille. The fish and potatoes can be added to the soup bowl or enjoyed separately on a plate.

A PROPER BOUILLABAISSE
Chris Made His Differently in New Orleans Than He Did in France

I SO LOVED BOUILLABAISSE, which my Chef Chris Kerageorgiou knew—as well as he knew that I'd never seen a real bouillabaisse until I made it with him in his backyard, just minutes from his childhood home in Port-St.-Louis. This soup must be prepared with what the home cook has—no fancy gadgets, just a food mill, a big pot, knives and spoons, mortar and pestle. "Dis is how ma mamma did it, Baby," he'd tell me as he went about his work. Off to the market we'd go, tasting, smelling, talking, laughing, and savoring in anticipation of the meal to come.

It's been said that the first bouillabaisse was served by Venus to Vulcan, and because those gods seemed reluctant to share their immortal recipe with us mere mortals, we've been toying with the recipe ever since. But it was the hardy people of Provence who created the classic bouillabaisse around the port of Marseille, precisely where Chef Chris developed his love for this meal. Simply, bouillabaisse is a fish stew, made from the inexpensive fish of the rocky Mediterranean coastline, bony fish that when cooked slowly add their gelatinous quality to the broth. By definition, the *bouill* (*bouillir* = to boil) comes from ceremoniously boiling the broth with onions, garlic, fennel, tomatoes, saffron, and orange peel in a large pot with enough heft to retain a constant heat. *Abaisse* happens later, when the boney fish are plunged into the boiling broth, thus cooling it down (*abaisser* = to lower) and momentarily ceasing the boil. The number of fish used depends upon the number of guests to be served—the more people, the greater the variety. Like the gumbo of my hometown, bouillabaisse is reserved for large social gatherings. Since many different seafoods are used, much care is given to making sure that by the time the stew is finished each fish is cooked perfectly. This is why the larger fish are generally added first, and any shellfish go into the pot just before serving.

No two bouillabaisses are alike and even Chris made his differently in New Orleans than he did in France; near the Mediterranean, his would always contain *rascasse* (scorpion fish) and conger eel. At La Provence, he'd use thick chunks of monkfish, along with mussels, clams, squid, and shrimp. Just as with our gumbo, you'll seldom find two folks who agree on bouillabaisse and in no time heated discussions will break out. One thing people pretty much do agree on is that the stew is served in two separate courses: First comes the broth the seafood was cooked in, perfumed with all the delicious Provençal flavors you'd expect, and served with croutons—slices of day-old baguette toasted and rubbed with raw garlic and drizzled with olive oil. These garlicky croutons are the vessel for the incredibly flavorful rouille, the garlic mayonnaise seasoned with harissa or crushed chile peppers and thinned with saffron-stained broth. Often a grated mountain of Gruyère cheese is sprinkled on top.

After much ceremony and several helpings of broth, it's time to partake in the second course: the prized fish that have slow-cooked so that the flesh easily pulls off the bone, along with potatoes, steamed or slowly simmered in the delicious broth. More rouille accompanies the impressive platter of seafood. Chris's table was anything but orderly. Once the bouillabaisse was served, everyone noisily helped themselves from platters of poached seafood and bowls of pungent rouille. There was plenty of well-chilled wine, as well as pastis poured from Ricard bottles into glasses topped off with ice water. Now that's living.

243

SAFFRON CRAB STEW

Serves 6–8

¼ cup olive oil

2 dozen blue crabs, crushed (see Alain's Soupe de Poissons, page 237)

1 leek, chopped

1 fennel bulb, chopped

1 carrot, peeled and chopped

4 cloves garlic, chopped

A few pinches red pepper flakes

2 pinches saffron

6 tomatoes, chopped, or 2 cups canned diced tomatoes

2 tablespoons tomato paste

1 cup white wine

2 sprigs fresh thyme

2 bay leaves

4 yellow potatoes, peeled and chopped

Peel of 1 orange

Salt

Freshly ground black pepper

Rouille (page 241)

Grated cheese such as Gruyère

THIS IS ONE OF MY LONGTIME favorite recipes, inspired by the original Soupe de Favouilles I brought back from Provence, but using blue crabs instead of the tiny Mediterranean crabs. I still get requests for this stew nearly 20 years later. The point of the food mill is to extract as much flavor from the shells as possible. If you don't have a food mill, just strain the soup.

1. Heat the oil in a large, heavy-bottomed pot over medium-high heat. Add the crushed crabs and stir until the shells turn red, about 10 minutes, toasting the crabs to bring out the flavor.

2. Add the leeks, fennel, carrots, garlic, pepper flakes, and saffron and cook, stirring occasionally, 3–5 minutes. Add the tomatoes and tomato paste and cook until the tomatoes are softened, about 10 minutes. Add the wine, thyme, bay leaves, and enough water to cover the crabs by about 1 inch and bring to a boil. Add the potatoes and orange peel. Reduce the heat to medium low and simmer about 1 hour. Discard the orange peel, bay leaf, and thyme sprigs.

3. Set up a food mill over a medium pot and grind the crab soup through the mill, discarding the ground shells as you work. Season the soup with salt and pepper. Serve the soup in bowls with the Rouille and cheese.

ALAIN'S BOUQUET GARNI

WE WERE DELIGHTED with the inventive way Alain Assaud wraps his aromatics to flavor a soup or a stew. Showing typical Provençal ingenuity, he makes sure that nothing goes to waste.

Take an outer leaf from a leek, one you'd normally discard, and wrap it around parsley, thyme, bay leaves, lavender, and any other fresh and dried herbs that appeal. Fold the leek frond over the herbs and tie it up with kitchen string. Pop the bouquet into the soup or braising pot.

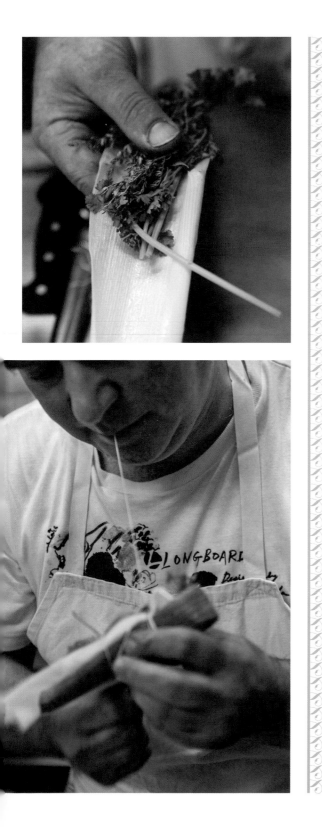

BOURRIDE OF MONKFISH

Serves 6

1 pound monkfish, cut into small pieces

3 tablespoons olive oil

2 cloves garlic, minced

1 sprig fresh thyme

Pinch cayenne pepper

1 medium leek, chopped

1 small fennel bulb, chopped

4½ cups Basic Fish Stock (page 40)

1 bay leaf

1 cup Aïoli (page 181)

Salt

BOURRIDE IS AKIN TO bouillabaisse—a main course fish stew—but instead of tomatoes, it is based on a luscious marriage of fish stock and Aïoli. The monkfish is marinated in olive oil, thyme, and garlic and poached in fish stock at the last minute, then the stock is thickened with Aïoli. You'll need a crusty loaf of bread to soak up the delicious flavors.

1. Marinate the monkfish with 2 tablespoons of the olive oil, half of the garlic, the thyme, and cayenne in a bowl for 30 minutes.

2. Heat the remaining tablespoon of oil in a large pot over medium-high heat. Add the leeks, fennel, and remaining garlic and cook, stirring, until the leeks and fennel are soft. Add the Fish Stock and bay leaf and bring to a boil. Reduce the heat to medium and simmer for 10–15 minutes.

3. With the pot at a very low simmer, add the monkfish and poach gently for another 10 minutes. Discard thyme and bay leaf.

4. Remove a cup of the broth to a bowl and whisk in the Aïoli. Stir back into the pot, mixing well. Season with salt. Serve in soup bowls, adding a few pieces of fish to the beautiful creamy broth.

BASIC VICHYSSOISE

Serves 6

1 tablespoon
olive oil

1 leek, chopped

2 cloves garlic,
crushed

2 large Yukon Gold
or yellow pota-
toes, peeled and
chopped

5 cups Basic Chicken
Stock (page 250)

½ cup heavy cream

1 sprig fresh thyme

1 bay leaf

Salt

Freshly ground
black pepper

1 tablespoon
chopped fresh
chives

THIS POTATO SOUP IS MY GO-TO BASE. It's the perfect starting point for Any Vegetable Soup (which I wrote about in *My Family Table*). I use it to make White Asparagus–Potato Soup (page 249), Watercress Soup (page 249), and its variation Chilled Sorrel Soup, as well as versions based on cauliflower, broccoli, asparagus, spinach, carrots...you name it.

1. Heat the oil in a medium pot over medium-high heat. Add the leeks and garlic and cook, stirring, until the leeks are softened but not browned, 3–5 minutes. Add the potatoes, Chicken Stock, cream, thyme, and bay leaf and bring to a boil. Reduce the heat and simmer for about 30 minutes. Season with salt and pepper.

2. Remove the thyme and bay leaf and, in batches, purée the soup in a blender, or use an immersion blender as below, right in the pot. Strain and serve, either chilled or warm, topped with chives.

WATERCRESS SOUP

Serves 6

1 bunch watercress, washed and chopped

2 green onions, chopped

1 clove garlic, peeled

½ cup (1 stick) butter

Salt

Freshly ground black pepper

Basic Vichyssoise (page 246)

THIS SOUP IS BEST SERVED just as the butter is stirred into the hot Vichyssoise in order to retain its delightful bright green color. I create a watercress compound butter to add to the soup. Compound butter of parsley, basil, or basil and tomato added to the creamy potato base makes an excellent soup as well.

1. Make the compound butter by combining the watercress, green onions, garlic, and butter in a blender along with a pinch of salt and pepper. Purée until smooth. Reserve and refrigerate the butter until ready to serve.

2. Heat the Vichyssoise in a medium pot over medium-high heat. Just before serving, stir the watercress butter into the soup and ladle into bowls.

CHILLED SORREL SOUP

Serves 6

Blanch and shock 1 bunch of spinach and 1 bunch of sorrel and purée with cold or hot Vichyssoise. Season with salt and pepper.

WHITE ASPARAGUS–POTATO SOUP

Serves 6

Basic Vichyssoise (page 246)

1 cup blanched white asparagus peels and trim

Squeeze of lemon

½ teaspoon sugar

Salt

Freshly ground black pepper

1 cup sliced cooked asparagus, for garnish

A LUSCIOUS BASE OF VICHYSSOISE enhances the delicate flavor of white asparagus. This is a soup to make for the brief and glorious moment white asparagus is in season. Since that vegetable is so special, I save every bit of the precious asparagus trimmings for the soup. Reserve a few of the cooked white asparagus as garnish for the soup.

1. In a medium pot, bring the Vichyssoise, white asparagus peels, lemon, and sugar to a boil. Season with salt and pepper. Purée the soup in a blender. Scatter a few sliced asparagus spears in each bowl.

249

BASIC VEAL STOCK

Makes about 6 cups

1 tablespoon
canola oil

2 large onions,
roughly chopped

2 carrots, roughly
chopped

1 stalk celery,
roughly chopped

3 cloves garlic,
crushed

1 bay leaf

1 sprig fresh thyme

1 teaspoon black
peppercorns

3 pounds veal bones
such as shanks,
halved

I NEVER MAKE A STRONG BEEF STOCK, preferring instead the viscosity, collagen, and more delicate flavor that comes from using veal bones. This Veal Stock is based on veal shanks.

1. In a large heavy-bottomed pot, heat the oil over medium-high heat. Add the onions, carrots, celery, garlic, bay leaf, thyme, and peppercorns, stirring until softened. Add the bones and cover with 12 cups cold water. Bring to a boil, reduce the heat, and simmer for 3 hours, skimming the foam periodically. Strain through a fine mesh strainer into a large bowl. The stock is ready to use, or chill and freeze for future soups and stews.

BASIC CHICKEN STOCK

Makes about 6 cups

2 carcasses roast
chicken

2 onions, peeled and
quartered

2 carrots, roughly
chopped

2 stalks celery,
roughly chopped

1 clove garlic,
crushed

1 sprig fresh thyme

1 bay leaf

½ teaspoon black
peppercorns

SAVE THE CARCASS from every chicken you roast—it's the foundation of a great chicken soup. I always have a few in my freezer for just this purpose.

1. Combine the chicken carcasses, onions, carrots, celery, garlic, thyme, bay leaf, and peppercorns in a large heavy-bottomed pot. Cover with 12 cups cold water and bring to a boil. With a spoon, skim and discard the foam that rises to the top. Reduce the heat to medium low and simmer until reduced by about half, about 3 hours. Strain the stock through a fine-mesh strainer over a large bowl. The stock is ready to use, or chill and freeze for future soups and stews.

CHICKEN CONSOMMÉ WITH CHIFFONADE OF CHIVE CRÊPES

Serves 6

1 onion, halved, rubbed with canola oil

FOR THE CONSOMMÉ

6 egg whites

1 leek, chopped

1 carrot, chopped

1 stalk celery, chopped

2 tomatoes, chopped

1 pound ground chicken breast

4 fresh parsley stems

1 sprig fresh thyme

1 bay leaf

½ teaspoon black peppercorns

6 cups Basic Chicken Stock (page 250)

Salt

FOR THE CRÊPES

½ cup milk

2 eggs

½ cup flour

½ teaspoon salt

2 tablespoons butter, melted, plus more for cooking the crêpes

2 tablespoons chopped fresh chives

THIS TRADITIONAL SOUP OF BADEN, where it's called *Flaedlesuppe,* pancake soup, gets its signature dark color from the deeply browned onion cooked with the broth. The chive crêpes absorb the beautiful consommé, giving them a noodle-like texture. I learned this method for making the purest, clearest consommé so many years ago from Karl-Josef. Ground turkey is a good substitute for the chicken. Karl-Josef serves Sabine and his daughters, Victoria and Christina, below.

1. I like to begin by making an onion *brûlé,* which means browning the onion halves in a cast iron skillet on high heat until they turn a deep mahogany color and are almost burnt. Set aside.

2. For the consommé, whisk the egg whites in a large bowl until frothy. Stir the leeks, carrots, celery, tomatoes, chicken, parsley, thyme, bay leaf, and peppercorns into the beaten whites until thoroughly combined. You're preparing an egg white raft to clarify the stock. Put the Chicken Stock in a large, heavy-bottomed pot, then add the browned onion and stir in the egg white mixture. Turn the heat to medium and bring to a simmer, stirring occasionally so the ingredients don't sink to the bottom.

3. As the stock heats, the egg white mixture will begin to coalesce. Stop stirring at this point. Reduce the heat to low and let the ingredients rise to the surface and form a large raft. Simmer for 30 minutes. Scoop a small hole in the center of the raft with the edge of a ladle and spoon the soup over the raft to moisten it and clarify the soup. Cook for another 30 minutes, occasionally ladling the soup over the raft.

4. Put a fine-mesh strainer over a large bowl. Working around the raft, ladle the clarified soup through the strainer. The resulting consommé should be beautiful—clear enough to see right through. Discard raft. Season with salt.

5. For the crêpe batter, combine the milk, eggs, and ½ cup water in a large bowl and whisk in the flour, salt, and butter until well mixed. Stir in the chives. Cover and chill the batter for about 15 minutes.

6. Melt 1 teaspoon butter in a small non-stick skillet over medium heat. Add about 3 tablespoons crêpe batter and swirl the pan to spread the batter over the bottom. Cook, turning once, until both sides are golden brown, about 2 minutes. Continue making crêpes, adding butter to the pan, until all the batter is used. Stack the crêpes on a plate and cut them into thin strips.

7. Ladle the consommé into hot bowls and sprinkle with the sliced crêpes.

253

MAKING CONSOMMÉ

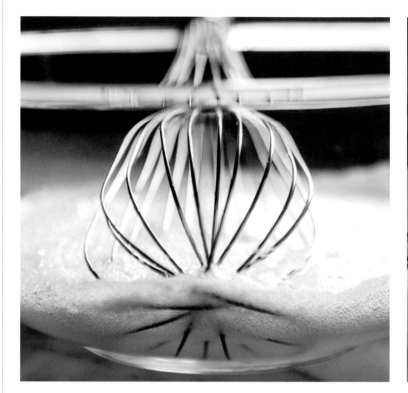

1. Whisk very cold egg whites in a large bowl. Either add solids to this bowl, or follow step 2.

2. Pour the frothy egg whites into a bowl of shredded leeks, carrots, celery, chopped tomatoes, and ground chicken.

3. Stir the mixture well and spoon it into the cold stock. Keep stirring until the soup comes to a low simmer.

4. Once the raft has formed, make a hole and spoon the soup over the raft to moisten it and clarify the soup.

5. Ladle the soup from the pot through the hole in the raft (careful not to disturb it) into a fine-mesh strainer set over a large bowl. The resulting consommé should be clear enough to see right through. Discard raft.

CHILLED SHELLFISH & TOMATO CONSOMMÉ WITH AVOCADO

Serves 6

FOR THE
CONSOMMÉ

2 tablespoons
olive oil

1 cup shrimp heads
and shells

1 teaspoon red
pepper flakes

1 large leek, chopped

1 stalk celery,
chopped

4 cloves garlic,
chopped

6 large tomatoes,
chopped

6 egg whites

12 cups Basic Shrimp
Stock (page 49)

12 large shrimp,
peeled, deveined,
and cooked

½ cup picked lump
crab meat

Salt

1 avocado, pitted and
chopped

1 cup cherry
tomatoes, halved

Leaves from
2 sprigs fresh basil

I LIKE TO SERVE THIS SOUP as a chilled first course, but it's equally good served warm. When the consommé is poured over the garnish of shrimp, crab, avocado, and cherry tomatoes, it creates a colorful mosaic of flavors and textures.

1. For the consommé, heat the oil in a large, heavy-bottomed pot over medium-high heat. Add the shrimp heads and shells and pepper flakes and toast until the shells turn red, about 5 minutes. Add the leeks, celery, and garlic and cook until softened, 5–7 minutes. Reduce the heat to medium low and add chopped tomatoes.

2. Whisk the egg whites in a large bowl until frothy. Stir the shrimp shell mixture into the beaten egg whites until thoroughly combined. You're preparing an egg white raft to clarify the stock. Put the Shrimp Stock in a large pot and stir in the egg white mixture. Turn the heat to medium and bring to a simmer, stirring occasionally so the ingredients don't sink to the bottom.

3. As the stock heats, the egg white mixture will begin to coalesce. Stop stirring at this point. Reduce the heat to low and let the ingredients rise to the surface and form a large raft. Simmer for 30 minutes. Scoop a small hole in the center of the raft with the edge of a ladle and spoon the soup over the raft to moisten it and clarify the soup. Cook for another 30 minutes, occasionally ladling the soup over the raft.

4. Put a fine-mesh strainer over a large bowl. Working around the raft, ladle the clarified soup through the strainer. The consommé should

be beautiful—clear enough to see right through. Discard raft. Refrigerate for several hours.

5. To serve, season with a touch of salt. Distribute the shrimp, crab, avocado, and tomatoes among 6 soup bowls. Pour in the consommé and garnish with basil leaves.

WILD GAME CONSOMMÉ WITH CÈPES & SAGE

Serves 6

FOR THE CONSOMMÉ

6 egg whites

1 leek, chopped

1 carrot, chopped

1 stalk celery, chopped

1 small tomato, chopped

1 pound ground lean game meat

4 fresh parsley stems

1 sprig fresh thyme

1 bay leaf

½ teaspoon black peppercorns

6 cups Basic Chicken Stock (page 250)

Salt

FOR THE MUSHROOMS

1 tablespoon olive oil

3 porcini mushrooms, or 12 chanterelles or oyster mushrooms, cleaned and sliced

Leaves from 1 sprig fresh sage, thinly sliced

Salt

IF YOU HAVE ACCESS TO WILD GAME, this is a wonderful way to use it. Otherwise, you can surely find lean meat from domestic rabbit, duck, venison, or pheasant and have it ground by your butcher for this amazingly flavorful soup. Lean meat really matters here. As pictured above, clarified consommé before cèpes are added.

1. For the consommé, whisk the egg whites in a large bowl until frothy. Stir in the leeks, carrots, celery, tomatoes, ground meat, parsley, thyme, bay leaf, and peppercorns until thoroughly combined. You're preparing an egg white raft to clarify the stock. Put the chicken stock in a medium pot and stir in the egg white mixture. Turn the heat to medium and bring to a simmer, stirring occasionally so the ingredients don't sink to the bottom.

2. As the stock heats, the egg white mixture will begin to coalesce. Stop stirring at this point. Reduce the heat to low and let the ingredients rise to the surface and form a large raft. Simmer for 30 minutes. Scoop a small hole in the center of the raft with the edge of a ladle, and spoon the soup over the raft to moisten it and clarify the soup. Cook for another 30 minutes, occasionally ladling the soup over the raft.

3. Put a fine-mesh strainer over a large bowl. Working around the raft, ladle the clarified soup through the strainer. The resulting consommé should be beautiful— clear enough to see right through. Discard raft. Season with salt.

4. For the mushrooms, heat the olive oil in a medium skillet over high heat. Add the mushrooms and quickly sauté for about 1 minute. Stir in the sage and season with salt. Top each bowl of consommé with the sautéed mushrooms.

257

VEAL CONSOMMÉ WITH MARROW DUMPLINGS

Serves 6

FOR THE MARROW DUMPLINGS

1 pound marrow bones

1¼ cups fresh bread crumbs

¼ cup flour, plus more for dusting

2 eggs

2 tablespoons milk

1 tablespoon chopped fresh chives

FOR THE CONSOMMÉ

6 egg whites

1 leek, chopped

1 carrot, chopped

1 stalk celery, chopped

1 small tomato, chopped

1 pound lean ground beef

4 sprigs fresh parsley

1 sprig fresh thyme

1 bay leaf

½ teaspoon black peppercorns

6 cups Basic Veal Stock (page 250)

Salt

THOUGH THIS RECIPE MAY SEEM A BIT COMPLICATED, it is the essence of a great beef flavor: a celebration of good, fortified, clarified beef soup floating with marrow dumplings. In place of beef, I'll often use ground venison, wild boar, or any game fowl. When it comes to consommé, it can be made a day or two in advance, kept in the fridge, and reheated as you need it.

1. For the marrow dumplings, in a medium pot of steaming salted water, poach the bones for 2 minutes. Remove the bones from the water, pop the marrow onto a cutting board, and roughly chop. You should have about ½ cup marrow.

2. Put the marrow in a medium mixing bowl and add the bread crumbs, flour, eggs, milk, and chives. Knead the mixture until a soft dough forms. Dust your hands with flour and roll the dough into small, quarter-sized balls. Place on a plate and refrigerate while you make the consommé.

3. For the consommé, whisk the egg whites in a large bowl until frothy. Stir the leeks, carrots, celery, tomatoes, ground beef, parsley, thyme, bay leaf, and peppercorns into the beaten egg whites until thoroughly combined. You're preparing an egg white raft to clarify the stock. Put the Veal Stock in a medium pot and stir in the egg white mixture. Turn the heat to medium and bring to a simmer, stirring occasionally so the ingredients don't sink to the bottom.

4. As the stock heats, the egg white mixture will begin to coalesce. Stop stirring at this point. Reduce the heat to low and let the ingredients rise to the surface and form a large raft. Simmer for 30 minutes. Scoop a small hole in the center of the raft with the edge of a ladle and spoon the soup over the raft to moisten it and clarify the soup. Cook for another 30 minutes, occasionally ladling the soup over the raft.

5. Put a fine-mesh strainer over a large bowl. Working around the raft, ladle the clarified soup through the strainer. The resulting consommé should be beautiful—clear enough to see right through. Discard raft. Season with salt.

6. When you're ready to serve the consommé, bring a medium pot of salted water to a boil. Reduce the heat to low and drop in the dumplings. Once the dumplings rise to the top, cook another 30 seconds then remove with a slotted spoon and drain on paper towels. Serve the dumplings in bowls of the hot consommé.

Fruit, Nuts

& Cheese

FEW THOUGHTS BRING a readier grin to my face than the image of Edel Neary, a cute and very shy Irish pastry chef in Karl-Josef's kitchen at the Spielweg, and the ribbing she got from the male-dominated staff about an upcoming holiday at a topless French beach. As the Irish daughter of a sergeant of the guard, she'd grown up proper and well-protected; this was the first time Edel had ever been away from her hometown other than studying pastry in Galway. She found herself in the Black Forest on an educational mission formed to strengthen the Irish culinary system, cross-training with chefs from other nations. Quiet and reserved, Edel was considerably talented in pastry, but as a young woman in the kitchen, she was ferociously picked on by our

PATISSERIES ABOUND in charming St.-Rémy, left. Overleaf, signature Provençal sweets, from left, puffy meringue navets, Luberon fruit liqueurs, *calissons* from Aix-en-Provence, Apt candied fruit, Montélimar nougats.

263

"Edel had a trick of using dried fruits in her fresh fruit tarts, so the flavorful fruit absorbs the fruit juices and adds great texture."

WITH JENIFER AND EDEL on a weekend in Andechs, Bavaria, 1993, above. The streets of nearby Staufen, known for everything fruit, right.

French sous chef and the many German *commis*. My fellow cooks never understood the fondness most Americans have for the Irish, or that being from the South meant chivalry was expected. Hence, I found myself in the position of big brother and protector of this Irish lady. And so it was that Edel became like part of our family, spending many off hours and vacations with Jenifer and me.

This was long before cell phones and e-mail were commonplace, and Jenifer's father, Patrick Berrigan, would regularly fax us articles about food and travel. One day, before our vacation to the South of France, Patrick sent us a piece from the *New York Times* on Bandol, its food, its wine, and its topless beaches! All faxes normally passed through the hands of Karl-Josef, and such a piece wouldn't have gotten much reaction, but since Edel was to accompany us on our vacation, the thought of that precious, shy, and very proper baker thrown to the hedonistic and naked French sent him into fits of hysterical laughter. Chef immediately called the entire kitchen together for a pre-dinner service huddle and decreed that our Edel would now be nicknamed "Topless."

A few days later, Topless in tow, we arrived at our *gîte rural*, a smallish former farmhouse right smack in the midst of apricot, fig, mirabelle, apple, and pear orchards, rimmed with ancient hedges of blueberries and black-

berries. The farm, looking as if it were being swallowed up by the jagged rocks of the foothills of the nearby Alpilles and a short hop to the beach, was just minutes from one of my favorite restaurants, l'Oustau de Baumanière and the citadel of Les Baux in the Val d'Enfer—the Valley of Hell. This vacation would be our last hoorah before returning home to the States. With my work visa expiring and our return to reality imminent, we called this our dessert course—just one last little bit of sweetness before "real work" and responsibilities of life would overtake us. We planned a week full of shopping at local markets, cooking, and playing *pétanque*.

We shared the farmhouse with Jenifer's parents, Pat and Barbara Berrigan, as well as her sister Mary, Uncle Kurt, and Linda Sins, all raucous New Orleaneans with a singular focus: devour Provence. Each morning Edel and I would create a menu as we wandered through the orchard, beginning with dessert. We decided to always let the fruit dictate what we'd make. Normally, we chefs

264

EDEL would have made a plum tart like this one, above, at the Spielweg. At Schladerer, Staufen's premium distiller of fruit brandies (or schnapps), pears like these, left, are destined for Williams pear brandy, right.

ALAIN ASSAUD'S dessert at his St.-Rémy restaurant: Lemon Biscuits with Mirabelle Ice Cream and Berries. Navets and fougasses in a bakery, right.

tend to focus on cooking strictly savory foods, which are more forgiving. Yet, I was groomed by all-around pros like Chef Chris, Karl-Josef, and others who demanded that cooks master baking and pastry. But this was really special—a pastry vacation in a Provençal orchard with our own phenomenal pastry chef, Topless Neary.

Though she was born Irish, Edel's style was completely French; she had a grandmother's fine touch—refined yet approachable. She used no precious ingredients, which made her desserts all the more precious indeed. Butter, cream, sugar, and eggs played a supporting role to the fruit that starred at every meal. Once settled into our little *mas*, I turned to opening bottles of Coteaux d'Aix-en-Provence, while Topless went off to inspect the apricots, which, a few bottles later, appeared in the form of a large apricot clafoutis perfumed with lavender honey.

Decades afterward, I have absolutely no recollection of the dishes I made for our sumptuous lunches and dinners. But I do vividly recall the creaminess of Edel's clafoutis, the firmness of each apricot. (I also vividly remember my midnight strolls through the orchards, wine bottle in hand, and my amazement at the sheer

numbers of *sanglier*—wild boar—foraging for fallen fruit under the stars. I was even more amazed when I learned that Provençal hunters would stalk them at night. I'd been so naïve wandering around in the dark, drinking wine; I could have been mistaken for a wild pig!)

Topless had a gift with rustic tarts, too, preparing pie dough as if she were a silversmith, meticulously cutting each diamond-sized nugget of butter into the flour so that it did not melt. This resulted in fine granules that looked like coarse semolina, which, when a few drops of ice cold water were mixed in, become a pliable ball of sweet buttery goodness. When she rolled and baked that dough, it tasted more like butter cookies than my own pie dough. She'd make another version of the dough using a couple parts flour, blended with a part of hazelnut or almond flour, which not only added the obvious nut flavor, but a crumbly texture that melted on the palate. Edel used her doughs interchangeably, for free form rustic tarts or fancier ones made in a fluted tart mold.

Our rented farmhouse had little in the way of cooking, much less baking equipment, so we'd make our tarts rustic and free form: tossing our fresh-picked plums,

266

"Topless had a gift with rustic tarts, too, making pie dough like a silversmith, cutting diamond-shaped pieces of butter into the flour."

berries, or apricots with sugar beaten to a fluffy cream with a pinch of butter and egg, which slightly bound the fruit juices into what I affectionately called "sticky goo," then wrapping it all in sweet dough. Our goo allowed the pie dough to bake crisply instead of becoming soggy. I loved the way Edel would create a kind of nutty sweet streusel topping with almonds, hazelnuts, walnuts, pine nuts, or any combination of the above. The nuts, tossed with brown sugar, nut flour, and butter with a touch of cinnamon would be sprinkled over a tart about half-way through baking so that by the time the nuts were perfectly browned, the dough would be golden and delicious. Another of Edel's tricks was to use dried fruit or berries in her fresh fruit tarts, letting the intensely flavored dried fruit absorb the juices of the fresh fruit— at the same time adding great texture and fortifying the flavor. I've since borrowed her idea for all sorts of dishes both savory and sweet.

Not only was my style of cooking influenced by the rigors of cooking and baking in the strictly regimented brigades of both Karl-Josef and my beloved Chef Chris, but my passion for desserts came from having the time to experiment with the delicious ingredients from my little corner of Provence under the tutelage of Topless Neary. That time spent cooking and baking would later become the foundation for the way I cook and bake at home. I love desserts that are approachable, simple yet elegant and delectable, allowing the beauty of perfect ingredients like the freshest fruit, yard eggs, nuts, and chocolate to be elevated through passion and respect. And to this day, whenever I walk into my kitchen to make one of them, I think of Topless Neary. And I smile.

MASTER CHEESEMAKER on a tiny back street of St.-Rémy, top, elegant logs of soft, fresh chèvre are fes-tooned with wild herbs, above.

267

RAINBOW OF FLAVORS pots de crème from top: Espresso, Strawberry-Mint, Dark Chocolate, Meyer Lemon, and more Espresso.

BASIC POT DE CRÈME

Makes 6

1 cup whole milk

1 cup heavy cream

½ cup sugar

Pinch salt

1 teaspoon vanilla
extract

6 egg yolks

THIS DESSERT IS A LOVELY French custard, much lighter and more delicate than a crème brûlée or a flan, which is why it's served in the container it's baked in. I find the pots charming, and flavor the basic custard with a variety of fruits and sweets, and toppings of strawberries, chocolate, mint, walnuts, lemon zest, and pistachios.

1. Preheat the oven to 350°. Heat the milk, cream, sugar, and salt in a small saucepan over medium-high heat, stirring, until it comes to a boil. Remove from the heat and stir in the vanilla.

2. Whisk the yolks in a medium bowl. Add small amounts of the hot cream, whisking, until all the cream is incorporated.

3. Pour the custard into 6 pots de crème and set in a roasting pan lined with a dishtowel. Add enough hot water to reach halfway up the cups and cover the pan with foil. Bake until the custards are set, about 30 minutes. Cool, then refrigerate overnight before serving.

MEYER LEMON POT DE CRÈME

Add 2 tablespoons grated Meyer lemon zest to the milk and cream as it heats.

DARK CHOCOLATE POT DE CRÈME

Add 4 ounces chopped dark chocolate to the milk and cream as it heats. Be careful not to let the mixture boil, you just want to melt the chocolate.

STRAWBERRY-MINT POT DE CRÈME

Add 1 cup roughly chopped strawberries, 10 sprigs mint, and 2 additional tablespoons sugar to the milk and cream as it heats. Strain the custard before filling the cups.

PISTACHIO POT DE CRÈME

Purée 1 cup shelled pistachios in a food processor, then add them to the milk and cream as it heats. Strain the custard before filling the cups.

ESPRESSO POT DE CRÈME

Add ¼ cup ground espresso coffee beans to the milk and cream as it heats. Strain the custard before filling the cups.

PEACHES WITH MUSCAT DE BEAUMES-DE-VENISE

Serves 8

8 ripe peaches, pitted and quartered

1 cup Muscat de Beaumes-de-Venise

Leaves from 4 sprigs fresh mint

THE DISTINCTIVE SWEET WINE from the Provençal town of Beaumes-de-Venise has tones of honey and lavender; it is just about perfect poured over the ripest peaches. I look for any excuse to make this simple dessert in the summer.

1. Put the peaches in a large bowl. Add the wine, toss, and marinate for 30 minutes.

Serve with the mint leaves and tiny glasses of Beaumes-de-Venise.

QUINCE TART WITH DRIED CHERRIES

Serves 6–8

2 tablespoons butter

4 quinces, peeled and sliced

½ cup sugar

1 cup dried cherries

Basic Sweet Tart Dough (page 278)

QUINCES HAVE A BEAUTIFUL, ALMOST FLORAL AROMA when cooked. I like to soften them in a pan, then add dried cherries to absorb all their luscious juices, giving this tart its distinctive sweet-and-sour flavor.

1. Combine the butter, quinces, sugar, and ½ cup water in a medium saucepan. Bring to a boil over medium heat, reduce the heat, and simmer about 20 minutes. Stir in the cherries and let cool while you work on the dough.

2. Preheat the oven to 350°. Roll the Tart Dough on a well-floured surface into a large circle a little less than ¼ inch thick. Line a pie pan with the dough, and trim excess dough.

3. Pour the cooled filling into the pie shell. Bake until the crust is golden brown and the quince is tender, about 40 minutes.

1. In a large bowl, lightly beat the eggs and whisk in the milk to form an airy mixture.

2. Stream in the sugar, vanilla, and melted butter until the sugar is dissolved, scraping down the sides of the bowl.

3. Slowly whisk in the flour just until the clumps break up and a smooth batter forms. Don't overwork the batter.

4. Pour the entire bowl of batter into a large, seasoned cast iron skillet or pie pan.

1 cup whole milk

3 eggs

½ cup sugar

1 teaspoon vanilla extract

2 tablespoons butter, melted

½ cup all-purpose flour

BASIC CLAFOUTIS

Serves 4–6

APPROACH THE CLAFOUTIS BATTER as if you're making waffles! It's no more complicated than that. This recipe resonates with me because it is so simple and versatile and, at the same time, elegant. Most often I make a clafoutis in a black cast iron skillet or heavy pie pan because they retain the heat well. You can certainly use individual ramekins, a tart mold, or even a crêpe pan.

When you bake a clafoutis, it will puff up like a little soufflé, browned on the edges, but creamy within. I try to serve it immediately, because it will inevitably fall and deflate—but not to worry: This *will* happen and it's just as delicious anyway. If you understand this basic batter, the sky's the limit: it's a perfect blank canvas for almost any fruit you can think of: from choppable fruits like mango and banana, to cherries preserved in brandy. It's a recipe to draw upon all the year long. Variations follow, but here's the basic batter.

1. Preheat the oven to 325°. In a large bowl, whisk together the milk, eggs, sugar, vanilla, and butter until the sugar is dissolved. Add the flour and whisk until smooth. Pour the batter into a cast iron skillet or pie pan.

2. Now add your favorite fruit or flavoring (Concord Grape, page 275; Cherry, page 275; Pear with Eau de Vie, page 276; Milk Chocolate & Hazelnut, page 277). Bake until the clafoutis is beautifully puffed and golden, 35–40 minutes. Serve immediately.

5. Now's the time to add whatever fruit or nuts you like to the batter. Here, we crush the grapes for more flavor.

CONCORD GRAPE CLAFOUTIS
Once the batter is in the skillet, scatter 2 cups slightly crushed Concord or other black or red grapes on top.

CHERRY CLAFOUTIS
Scatter 2 cups pitted cherries onto the batter once it's poured into pie plates.

PEAR CLAFOUTIS WITH PEAR EAU DE VIE

Core 1 ripe pear and cut into pieces. Pour the batter into the skillet and top with the pear pieces. Bake. Drizzle with 2 tablespoons eau de vie and serve immediately.

MILK CHOCOLATE & HAZELNUT CLAFOUTIS

Melt 1 cup chopped milk chocolate in a large mixing bowl set above a simmering pot of water. Fold in the clafoutis batter until smooth and fully incorporated. Pour into a skillet or pie plate, sprinkle with ¼ cup coarsely chopped hazelnuts, and bake.

BASIC SWEET TART DOUGH

Makes enough for at least 1 large tart

½ cup (1 stick) cold butter, cut into pieces

2¼ cups all-purpose flour, plus more for rolling

⅓ cup sugar

¼ cup milk

1 egg

1 teaspoon grated lemon zest

1 teaspoon salt

THIS IS EDEL'S FAMOUS RECIPE, an easy dough that I keep on hand in the freezer so all I have to do is pull it out and 30 minutes later I have a perfect French *pâte sucrée*. Sugar-cookie sweet and crumbly, it lends itself to any sweet pie or tart recipe. I like the feel of making the dough by hand, but use a food processor if you prefer.

1. In a large mixing bowl, cut the cold butter into the flour until the flour has the consistency of semolina. Add the sugar, milk, egg, zest, and salt and mix by hand until a crumbly dough is formed. Shape the dough into a ball, wrap in plastic wrap, and refrigerate for at least an hour before using, or freeze for later use.

BROWN BUTTER–CARAMEL TART WITH BANANAS & PISTACHIOS

Serves 8

½ cup (1 stick) butter, plus 1 tablespoon softened butter for the pan

Basic Sweet Tart Dough (above)

3 eggs

1 cup sugar

¼ cup all-purpose flour

1 teaspoon vanilla extract

Pinch salt

3 bananas, peeled and sliced

½ cup shelled pistachios, whole and halved

A CARAMEL TART IS ONE OF THOSE DESSERTS that intrigued me as I was learning pastry and becoming a chef. I marveled at how adaptable the recipe is to so many different ingredients, both fruits and nuts, whatever's in season. Try making it with figs or the delicate little mirabelle plums instead of the bananas, and pecans or walnuts instead of pistachios.

1. Preheat the oven to 350°. Brush a 10-inch tart pan or pie dish with the 1 tablespoon softened butter and dust with flour. Roll the Tart Dough on a well-floured surface until it's ¼ inch thick. Line the tart pan with the dough, and trim excess dough.

2. Melt the ½ cup butter in a small sauce-pan over low heat and simmer until it turns amber, 10–12 minutes. With a hand or stand mixer, beat the eggs and sugar until fluffy and pale yellow. Slowly add the browned butter, flour, vanilla, and salt and beat until smooth.

3. Layer the bananas on the bottom of the tart shell. Spoon in the filling and spread on top of the bananas. Bake the tart about 20 minutes, then top with the pistachios. Return to the oven and bake until the top is golden brown, 20–25 minutes.

FRUIT COUNTRY: The fertile plains that border the Rhine near the Spielweg are some of the warmest places in Germany, in both senses. This, our perfect apple tree, eloquently tells the story.

APPLE & PEAR TART WITH WALNUTS

Serves 8–10

Basic Sweet Tart
Dough (page 278)

3-4 Gravensteins, Honeycrisps, or other tart apples, peeled, cored, and cubed

2 Bosc pears, cored and cubed

½ cup dark brown sugar

½ cup butter (1 stick) cut into pieces

½ cup walnuts, toasted and roughly chopped

½ teaspoon ground cinnamon

1 tablespoon lemon juice

USE WHATEVER COMBINATION OF APPLES, PEARS, AND EVEN QUINCE that you have on hand. I like to leave the skin on some of the fruit to add texture to the tart.

1. Preheat the oven to 350°. On a well-floured surface, roll the Tart Dough into a large oval a little less than ¼ inch thick. Transfer onto a baking pan.

2. In a large bowl, toss the apples and pears with the brown sugar. Add the butter and toss again. Add the walnuts, cinnamon, and lemon juice and toss well.

3. Mound the fruit and walnut mixture on top of the dough and wrap the dough over the fruit, covering most of it. Bake until the crust is golden brown, about 1 hour. Remove and cool a bit before serving.

1. Start with the crispest, freshest apples and pears you can find. Leave some of the skin on the fruit as you peel.

2. Slice the apples and pears from the core into wedges and cut into even-sized chunks.

3. Transfer the cut-up fruit to a large bowl and add the dark brown sugar. Toss to mix well.

4. Pinch 1-inch chunks of cold butter into the sugary fruit and toss again to mix well.

7. On a clean, lightly floured surface, roll out the Sweet Tart Dough into a large oval.

8. Gently transfer the rolled dough onto a rimmed baking pan and heap the fruit mixture in the center.

5. Add toasted and roughly chopped walnuts or other nuts to the fruit mixture. Mix again.

6. For more flavor, add cinnamon and lemon juice and toss again with your hands.

9. With your fingers, pull up the dough until it overlaps the fruit, gently folding as you go.

10. Crimp the dough with your fingertips to seal in the juices and form a wrapping for the fruit.

BLUEBERRY TART

Serves 8–10

4 tablespoons butter, plus 1 tablespoon softened butter for the pan

Basic Sweet Tart Dough (page 278)

1 egg, beaten

2 tablespoons lemon juice

Pinch salt

¾ cup sugar

1 cup all-purpose flour

5 cups blueberries

THIS PIE CAN BE MADE WITH ALMOST ANY FRESH BERRIES such as blackberries, raspberries, strawberries, or a combination of all of the above.

1. Preheat the oven to 350°. Brush a 10-inch fluted tart pan with the 1 tablespoon softened butter and dust with flour. Roll the Tart Dough on a well-floured surface until it's ¼ inch thick. Line the tart pan with the dough and trim excess dough.

2. Combine the egg, lemon juice, salt, ¼ cup of the sugar, and 1 teaspoon of the flour. Stir in the blueberries, then pour into the prepared tart shell. In a medium bowl, crumble together the remaining flour, ½ cup sugar, and 4 tablespoons butter into pea-sized clumps. Sprinkle on top of the berries. Bake until the topping is golden, 35–40 minutes.

PLUM TART WITH STREUSEL

Serves 8–10

4 tablespoons butter, plus 1 tablespoon softened butter for the pan

Basic Sweet Tart Dough (page 278)

1 egg

½ cup brown sugar

8-10 ripe Italian prune plums, quartered and pitted

1 cup all-purpose flour

½ cup granulated sugar

1 teaspoon cinnamon

Pinch salt

THINK OF *PFLAUMENKUCHEN* as the apple pie of the Black Forest region. It is such a staple that some cooks make it every day when the plums are in season.

1. Preheat the oven to 350°. Brush a 10-inch fluted tart pan with the 1 tablespoon softened butter and dust with flour. Roll the Tart Dough on a well-floured surface until it's ¼ inch thick. Line the tart pan with the dough, and trim excess dough.

2. In a medium bowl, beat the egg and brown sugar. Add the plums and toss. Arrange the plums in the tart shell with their pointed ends poking up. In a medium bowl, crumble together the 4 tablespoons butter, flour, granulated sugar, cinnamon, and salt into pea-sized clumps. Sprinkle over the plums. Bake until the plums are tender and the topping is golden, 35–40 minutes.

286

THE SECRET IS IN THE GRASS
Karl-Josef's Bergkäse Cheese Varies in Flavor with What the Cows Eat

IT IS AMAZING how much has been lost in just a generation or two as we have moved farther and farther away
from the farm. My father grew up on dairy farms, as his
father, highly educated in agriculture, managed dairy
and cattle farms for wealthy families. My pop, who broke
from tradition and opted to become a fighter pilot, still
held interests in farms, but we would *visit* the farm, not

work it as all my cousins did. So, in just one generation,
this Besh kid had lost a real attachment to the land.

In the first days working for Karl-Josef Fuchs, I realized
just how serious he was, not just about cooking and eating his food, but about its origins: the farmer, the pasture,
the sunlight, the snowfall. As a young chef all this was

new to me. When Karl-Josef took me into his *Käserei,* or cheese kitchen, to help him turn and brine-wash the cheeses he made, I wondered why he made cheese in such small batches. Why not ramp up production and market his phenomenal, nutty mountain cheeses to the world? Karl-Josef just looked at me, his deep brown eyes laughing as he explained that it was not about him, but about using only what the land provides in such limited abundance; "It's the grass that makes the cheese." He said that Spielweg cheese was different because it was made from live, unpasteurized milk that came only from *this* valley, where a special breed of small, sure-footed mountain cattle, the Hinterwälder, left, ate only the grass from the highest altitudes. To make his point, he'd show me firsthand.

In his olive drab Land Rover Defender, the chef drove me up the windy, narrow mountain road at terrifying speeds to pay his dairy farmer a visit. Near the tiptop of Schauinsland, a Black Forest peak famed among hikers and skiers, we stopped in to see the well-groomed, radiant Max, whose kindly nature and stately bearing reminded me of my grandfather. He exuded hospitality and, despite the early hour, immediately offered us Pflaumenschnaps, his homemade plum brandy. As the farmer walked us out onto a picturesque high mountain pasture, I saw the Hinterwälder cattle grazing on wildflowers and a carpet of grass, four inches deep, that smelled rich, floral, and herbaceous. The cows wore large bells that clanged about with their every move; that music, combined with the raw emotion of looking out over Switzerland, France, Germany, and, on a clear day, even Austria

(or so they say), made me realize once again what a special, fragile place this was. Each evening the cows are led off the mountain, back to the barn attached to the high-pitched, half-timbered, and meticulously kept home of the farmer. Each night or early morning the well-pampered cows are milked, fed barley and corn (both grown in the valley), and watered from the ever-flowing brook. Then they're led back up the mountain to a fresh buffet of sweet buttery grasses. Karl-Josef has me load a half dozen or so old-fashioned ten-gallon stainless milk jugs into the back of his truck as he offloads the empties. Farewells are exchanged. We're off to make cheese with my chef.

Karl-Josef's nutty and semi soft *Bergkäse* is a mountain cheese that, he explains, is as seasonal as the grass; as the grasses change so will the flavor and consistency of the cheese. It's important to capture the best milk from the perfect time of year. Early in spring before the snow melts on the mountaintop meadows, the fields at the lower elevations are ready for fertilizing with composted manure mixed with water and sprayed over the lovely pastures. Just weeks later the early grasses and herbs that emerge are more lush than anything that I've ever seen. As the weather warms, the cattle move farther up the mountain to find the perfect grass to make the perfect milk, which produces a cheese that can not be replicated. It is of this place, superb because of this land: the ample snowfall that soaks the ground and forces the grass into hibernation so that it will grow with vibrancy come spring; abundant sunshine; no fertilizer besides composted manure; and the short-legged cattle that have thrived on these steep slopes for centuries. I'd come to learn another important lesson that's served me so well over the years. Food and cooking is about balance, not only in its preparation but in its farming, too. Never again will I look at milk, cheese, or butter as mere pantry items; I revere them as gifts of the sun, the cows, and the grass.

Karl-Josef taught me what sustainable agriculture really means. Today, I have even been known to yell at my cooks who just leave a message with some anonymous purveyor to have their ingredients delivered. My Lord, I must be getting old, I think to myself. But it's true. Know your food, where it comes from and how it's grown: you will respect it and your cooking will shine.

FROM SWEET GRASS TO NUTTY CHEESE

Twice a Week in the Good Season, Karl-Josef Heads Up to the Dairy Farm

1. Twice a week in season, Karl-Josef loads empties into his Land Rover and picks up fresh milk from the farmer.

2. A ceremonial glass of plum schnapps is required, even at 8 am. An amiable dairy cow, above right. Max, the dairy farmer, right.

4. The curds are separated from the whey, above, and then strained out and portioned into cheese molds, right. The leftover whey is then clarified and made into fresh ricotta.

290

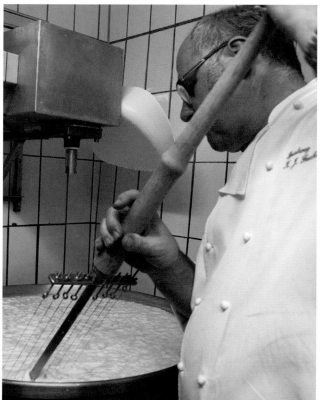

3. Back at the Spielweg, above, Karl-Josef pours the raw milk into a large copper vat to heat to about 100°, the temperature of the stomach of a dairy cow.

Then he adds the rennet to form curds in the milk. Right, Karl-Josef breaks up the curds with a cheese harp.

5. The wheels of *Bergkäse*, left, are aged from 60 to 90 days in a special room where they release their moisture. Above, Karl-Josef's cheese on sale in a shop in Freiburg.

WALTER & HIS EAGER APPRENTICE

I Learn a Pastry of Balance, Restraint, and Complexity

WALTER WAS THE SPIELWEG'S BAKER. He was not a fancy-pants pastry chef, but an interesting character whose hands could knead the perfect whole grain loaf of bread as easily as he could turn out every one of the traditional pastries that are consumed each day promptly at four o'clock with coffee, the German equivalent to tea time called *Kaffee und Kuchen*. It took me a while to understand that Walter was in fact teaching me a lesson in restraint with each of his pastries through his ability to balance perfectly the sweet with the tart, the crisp with the moist. A hefty slice of Walter's Schwarzwälder Kirschtorte—Black Forest Cake—consisted of five or six layers of chocolaty génoise drizzled with local Kirschwasser syrup and cherries preserved in cherry brandy. But this was then topped with freshly whipped farmer's sweet cream and paper thin shavings of dark chocolate that melted like snowflakes on the tongue. Each forkful was amazingly complex, given that the Kirshwasser-soaked cherries, which brought a balance to the chocolaty richness, were anything but sweet.

That cake was so delicious. But so was the quark cheesecake sliced thick and served warm from the oven. It was nestled in pastry dough so flaky it had to have been constructed from a pound of mountain butter that was yellow enough to color the crust a golden hue. A perfect amount of sweet offered a subtle contrast to the sour of quark whose texture was cloud-like. True perfection appeared in a strudel: layers and layers of crisp, newspaper-thin pastry that wrapped the perfectly soft, moist local apple wedges perfumed with local honey, nutmeg, and cinnamon, their caramel richness balanced by the tartness from the old world apple varieties.

Walter and I would eventually become friends; with loud public displays of what I assume was affection, he'd salute me and bark off John F. Kennedy's famous *"Ich bin ein Berliner."* I was touched by the time he took to visit with Jenifer, of whom he became quite fond. With a mischievous twinkle in his eye, he would

hand me sweet bits of cake, carefully wrapped in parchment, to take home to Jenifer, knowing she loved the trimmings from the quark cake as well as the ends and pieces of the strudel; these were never served to paying guests, but prized by us for breakfast.

WALTER'S CHEESECAKE

Serves 8–10

1 tablespoon butter, softened

Basic Sweet Tart Dough (page 278)

24 ounces cream cheese, at room temperature

1 cup sugar

½ teaspoon salt

4 eggs

¾ cup plain Greek yogurt

½ cup whole milk

1 tablespoon lemon juice

2 teaspoons vanilla extract

¼ cup all-purpose flour

THIS IS A VERSION OF THE BLACK FOREST QUARK CHEESECAKE that Walter made all those many years ago. Quark can be difficult to find: we've had excellent results using Greek yogurt and cream cheese instead.

1. Preheat the oven to 325°. Grease a 10-inch springform pan with the butter. Carefully roll the Tart Dough on a well-floured surface into a large flat sheet about ¼ inch thick. Fit the dough into the prepared pan, lining the edges of the pan and trimming the edges. The dough will most likely tear a bit, just be sure to patch it as you go with the trimmed dough. Refrigerate while you prepare the filling.

2. Using a hand or stand mixer, mix the cream cheese, sugar, and salt until smooth and fluffy, about 4 minutes. Add the eggs, mixing them in one at a time. Add the yogurt, milk, lemon juice, vanilla, and flour and mix until smooth.

3. Pour the batter into the dough shell. It will not reach all the way to the top, but that's fine since it will rise and expand as it bakes. Bake until golden brown, about 1 hour and 25 minutes. Cool the cake in the pan for 30 minutes. Remove the cake from the pan and continue to cool on a wire rack.

BLACK FOREST CAKE

Serves 8–10

2 cups all-purpose flour

¾ cup cocoa powder

1 teaspoon baking powder

1 teaspoon baking soda

½ teaspoon salt

¾ cup (1½ sticks) butter, plus more for the pans

1½ cups granulated sugar

2 eggs

1 teaspoon vanilla extract

1½ cups heavy cream

¼ cup confectioners' sugar

¼ cup Kirschwasser

1 (14-ounce) jar sour cherries, drained

1 bar semi-sweet chocolate, for shaving

THIS IS THE QUINTESSENTIAL Black Forest Cake that, no matter how fancy it looks, is nothing more than chocolate sponge cake perfumed with Kirschwasser and layered with sour cherries and whipped cream. There are thousands of recipes, every family has its own style. One refined version I love is made at Café Decker in Staufen near the Spielweg.

1. Preheat the oven to 350°. Butter and flour two 9-inch round cake pans.

2. In a large bowl, whisk together the flour, cocoa powder, baking powder, baking soda, and salt. In another bowl, beat the butter and granulated sugar together until light and fluffy. Beat in the eggs, one at a time, mixing thoroughly, and add the vanilla. Fold in the flour–cocoa powder mixture. Divide the batter between the two prepared pans. Bake until a toothpick inserted in the center comes out clean, 30–35 minutes. Cool the cakes in the pan for 15 minutes, then turn them onto wire racks to cool completely.

3. To assemble the cake, whip the cream with the confectioners' sugar until soft peaks form. Trim the tops of the cakes so that they're flat. Place one layer on a plate, drizzle with half of the Kirschwasser, and cover with the cherries. Spoon about a third of the whipped cream on top of the cherries. Place the second layer of cake on top and drizzle with the remaining Kirschwasser. Frost the cake on the top and sides with the remaining whipped cream. Just before serving, use a vegetable peeler to shave the chocolate over the cake.

SIPPING WITH Philipp Schladerer, right, the sixth generation of his family to run this premium artisanal distillery in Staufen, Germany near the Spielweg. Schladerer makes brandy from the fruit-rich region: apple, pear, cherry, grape, raspberry, mirabelle.

ACKNOWLEDGMENTS

I'D LIKE TO RECOGNIZE MY WIFE, Jenifer, who has given so selflessly to me. She so believed in my passion for discovery that twenty years ago she put her law career on hold so that I might work for pennies, learning from talented chefs and mentors around the globe. She saw what I often didn't: This journey and its amazing life lessons would make me a better chef. And a better man.

I will forever be indebted to the Berrigan, Conzen, Fuchs, Baur, and Béraud families for their delicious generosity and heartfelt hospitality over countless meals and lessons that have forever shaped my life and cooking.

Certainly there would be no book were it not for my dear Dorothy Kalins (with her gentle reminders and nudges), who produced and edited this, our third book together, and the heartfelt support of Kirsty Melville, president of Andrews McMeel. Both of them fervently believe that readers would find inspiration in *Cooking from the Heart*—Kirsty even thought up the title.

I am forever in awe of the passionate team that Dorothy brought together to make this collection of recipes and anecdotes so beautiful and so relevant: The photographer Maura McEvoy and her keen eye for the precise images to best articulate the story; Sue Li, our recipe editor, who persistently scribbled down every last step as we cooked, wrote, and tested our way through each recipe. I'm so thankful for the book's designer, Don Morris, and his ingenious ability to make each chapter flow to best tell my stories. Were it not for the groundwork in Europe painstakingly laid by Ariane Livaudais and her attention to every detail, we could never have accomplished so much. Thanks to our wonderful cooks, Will Smith, Blake Aguillard, and Miles Landrem, who traveled, shopped, and cooked with us. Thanks, too, to Emery Whalen and Kim Bourgault. And to filmmaker 'Uncle Roger' Sherman. Once again, big thanks to Jean Lucas, our loyal editor at Andrews McMeel, and to our eagle-eyed copy editor, Deri Reed, who helps make my thoughts clear.

And I am thankful for my parents, Imelda and Ted Besh, from whom I inherited wanderlust, and a love of people and food that bring us together.

OUR TEAM IN PROVENCE: Me and Jenifer, Roger Sherman, Blake Aguillard, Maura McEvoy, Ariane Livaudais, Dorothy Kalins, Will Smith, and Sue Li.

METRIC CONVERSIONS & EQUIVALENTS

APPROXIMATE METRIC EQUIVALENTS

Volume	Metric
¼ teaspoon	1 milliliter
½ teaspoon	2.5 milliliters
¾ teaspoon	4 milliliters
1 teaspoon	5 milliliters
1¼ teaspoons	6 milliliters
1½ teaspoons	7.5 milliliters
1¾ teaspoons	8.5 milliliters
2 teaspoons	10 milliliters
1 tablespoon (½ fluid ounce)	15 milliliters
2 tablespoons (1 fluid ounce)	30 milliliters
¼ cup	60 milliliters
⅓ cup	80 milliliters
½ cup (4 fluid ounces)	120 milliliters
⅔ cup	160 milliliters
¾ cup	180 milliliters
1 cup (8 fluid ounces)	240 milliliters
1¼ cups	300 milliliters
1½ cups (12 fluid ounces)	360 milliliters
1⅔ cups	400 milliliters
2 cups (1 pint)	460 milliliters
3 cups	700 milliliters
4 cups (1 quart)	0.95 liter
1 quart plus ¼ cup	1 liter
4 quarts (1 gallon)	3.8 liters

Weight	Metric
¼ ounce	7 grams
½ ounce	14 grams
¾ ounce	21 grams
1 ounce	28 grams
1¼ ounces	35 grams
1½ ounces	42.5 grams
1⅔ ounces	45 grams
2 ounces	57 grams
3 ounces	85 grams
4 ounces (¼ pound)	113 grams
5 ounces	142 grams
6 ounces	170 grams
7 ounces	198 grams
8 ounces (½ pound)	227 grams
16 ounces (1 pound)	454 grams
35.25 ounces (2.2 pounds)	1 kilogram

Length	Metric
⅛ inch	3 millimeters
¼ inch	6 millimeters
½ inch	1¼ centimeters
1 inch	2½ centimeters
2 inches	5 centimeters
2½ inches	6 centimeters
4 inches	10 cevtimeters
5 inches	13 centimeters
6 inches	15¼ centimeters
12 inches (1 foot)	30 centimeters

METRIC CONVERSION FORMULAS

To Convert	Multiply
Ounces to grams	Ounces by 28.35
Pounds to kilograms	Pounds by .454
Teaspoons to milliliters	Teaspoons by 4.93
Tablespoons to milliliters	Tablespoons by 14.79
Fluid ounces to milliliters	Fluid ounces by 29.57
Cups to milliliters	Cups by 236.59
Cups to liters	Cups by .236
Pints to liters	Pints by .473
Quarts to liters	Quarts by .946
Gallons to liters	Gallons by 3.785
Inches to centimeters	Inches by 2.54

OVEN TEMPERATURES

To convert Fahrenheit to Celsius, subtract 32 from Fahrenheit, multiply the result by 5, then divide by 9.

Description	Fahrenheit	Celsius	British Gas Mark
Very cool	200°	95°	0
Very cool	225°	110°	¼
Very cool	250°	120°	½
Cool	275°	135°	1
Cool	300°	150°	2
Warm	325°	165°	3
Moderate	350°	175°	4
Moderately hot	375°	190°	5
Fairly hot	400°	200°	6
Hot	425°	220°	7
Very hot	450°	230°	8
Very hot	475°	245°	9

COMMON INGREDIENTS & THEIR APPROXIMATE EQUIVALENTS

1 cup uncooked white rice = 185 grams

1 cup all-purpose flour = 140 grams

1 stick butter (4 ounces • ½ cup • 8 tablespoons) = 110 grams

1 cup butter (8 ounces • 2 sticks • 16 tablespoons) = 220 grams

1 cup brown sugar, firmly packed = 225 grams

1 cup granulated sugar = 200 grams

Information compiled from a variety of sources, including *Recipes into Type* by Joan Whitman and Dolores Simon (Newton, MA: Biscuit Books, 2000); *The New Food Lover's Companion* by Sharon Tyler Herbst (Hauppauge, NY: Barron's, 1995); and *Rosemary Brown's Big Kitchen Instruction Book* (Kansas City, MO: Andrews McMeel, 1998).

RESOURCES

HOTEL-RESTAURANT BLACK FOREST In *Chapters 1, 2, 3, 4 & 11*, you will see glorious examples of the cooking of my mentor, Karl-Josef Fuchs, and the warm hospitality of his wife, Sabine Fuchs. Karl-Josef is the fifth generation of his family to operate the Spielweg. Nestled in a gentle valley in the heart of the Black Forest in southern Germany, the Spielweg's restaurant and hotel are peerless in their commitment to local tradition and ingredients.

ROMANTIK-HOTEL SPIELWEG: Spielweg 61, 79244 Münstertal, Germany • +49 7636 7090 • www.spielweg.com.

WINERY BLACK FOREST A close friend and neighbor of Karl-Josef, Martin Wassmer makes fine wines from the grapes he grows in the rich region between the Black Forest and the Rhine.

MARTIN WASSMER: Am Sportplatz 3, 79189 Bad Krozingen-Schlatt, Germany • +49 7633 15292 • www.weingut-wassmer.de

FISH AND SEAFOOD I may have learned fish in Europe (*Chapter 2*), but at home, besides our excellent local purveyors, I rely on Rod Browne Mitchell to deliver the freshest fish, superb caviars, and smoked seafood. Based in Portland, Maine, Mitchell follows a family fishing tradition dating to the 1700s.

BROWNE TRADING CO.: Merrill's Wharf, 262 Commercial Street, Portland, ME • 800-944-7848, 207-775-7560 • www.brownetrading.com

RESTAURANT MULHOUSE Across the border from the Spielweg, Mulhouse has experienced massive restoration since the days when Jen and I would search the back streets for authentic Alsatian restaurants (*Chapter 5*). One of our favorites is still there.

WINSTUB HENRIETTE: 9 Rue Henriette, 68100 Mulhouse, France • +33 3 89 46 27 83

RESTAURANTS PROVENCE The small roadside bistros we loved (*Chapter 5*) have become popular and populated, but we think they're still worth the wait for a table on the terrasse.

BISTROT DU PARADOU: 57 Avenue de la Vallée des Baux, 13520 Paradou, France • +33 4 90 54 32 70

LA CANTONNADE: 10 Quai de la Fontaine, 30630 Goudargues, France • +33 4 66 82 30 65 • email lacantonnade@sfr.fr

HOUSE RENTAL PROVENCE We found the perfect house to rent as a base for production in Provence (*Chapters 6, 7 & 8*) probably just the way you would, by hunting online.

ONLY PROVENCE: www.francevacationvilla.com • 404-448-1565 • email info@only-provence.com

OLIVE OIL, HONEY, VINEGAR We could have brought back trunkfuls.

MONASTÈRE DE SOLAN: We fell hard for these artisanal products from a monastery near Uzès (*Chapter 9*). 30330 La Bastide d'Engras, France • +33 4 66 82 99 12 • www.monasteredesolan.com

MAUSSANE LES ALPILLES: Olive oil from a variety of producers in and around Maussane in the Vallée des Baux de Provence has AOC status and is said to be the best in France. Short of a trip directly there, which I heartily recommend, Maussane olive oil occasionally shows up on such websites as worldsfoods.com and zingermans.com.

RESTAURANT ST.-RÉMY Go for the Soupe de Poissons and Bouillabaisse, but any meal at the restaurant of my mentor and dear friend Alain Assaud (*Chapter 10*) is an authentic experience.

ALAIN ASSAUD: 13 Boulevard Marceau, 13210 St.-Rémy-de-Provence, France • +33 4 90 92 37 11

FISH AND SEAFOOD ST.-RÉMY Chef Alain Assaud's favorite fishmonger, specializing in Mediterranean fish and shellfish of the nearby Bouches-du-Rhône (*Chapter 10*).

POISSONNIERE ST. RÉMOISE: 22 Rue Carnot, 13210 St.-Rémy-de-Provence

SEDUCTIVE MARKET, left, on a square in Beaune. Patisserie Michel Marshall in St.-Rémy, above. Martin Wassmer makes fine wines in the Black Forest, right.

PATISSERIE ST.-RÉMY Alain Assaud's favorite, Marshall is a modernist pastry artist with the designation Maître Patissier de France.

MICHEL MARSHALL: 2 Place Joseph Hilaire, St.-Rémy-de-Provence, France • +33 4 08 99 10 34 03 • email contact@michelmarshall.fr

ARTISANAL FRUIT BRANDIES BLACK FOREST Philipp Schladerer is the sixth generation of his family to direct the artisanal distiller of the highest quality eaux de vie (such as Schwartzenwalder kirschwasser and Williams pear schnapps) in this fruit-rich country of the Black Forest (*Chapter 11*).

SCHLADERER: Schladererstrasse 1, 79219 Staufen im Breisgau, Germany • +49 7633 832-0 • www.Schladerer.de

KAFFE UND KÜCHEN BLACK FOREST Jenifer studied German in Staufen, and we would meet at the classic Café Decker for coffee and afternoon pastries. They still make a fine Black Forest Cake (page 294).

CONFISERIE CAFÉ DECKER: Hauptstrasse 70, 79219 Staufen im Breisgau, Germany • +49 7633 5316 • www.cafe-decker.de

CULINARY ANTIQUES NEW ORLEANS We used beautiful European objects throughout the book when we came home to photograph the process of cooking many of our recipes.

LUCULLUS CULINARY ANTIQUES, ARTS & OBJECTS: From table linen to silver serving pieces, copper cookware, and especially lovely French antique tableware, all are collected by proprietor Patrick Dunne and sold in his shop in the French Quarter.

610 Chartres Street, New Orleans, LA • 504-528-9620 • www.lucullusantiques.com

ANTIQUES DE PROVENCE: Cindy Nunez is an exemplary antiques dealer who represents the South of France in furniture, lighting, and accessories on Royal Street in New Orleans with shops at numbers 623, 619 and 611. • 504-529-4342 • www.antiquesdeprovencellc.com.

COOKWARE The company was established in 1830 by Ernest Mauviel in a small Normandy village. I love to use Mauviel copper, stainless, and aluminium cookware in my kitchen at home.

MAUVIEL USA: 802 Centerpoint Blvd., New Castle, DE • 302-326-4803 • www.mauvielusa.com

INDEX